The
LEATHER SLING
and
Shooting Positions

M/Sgt. JIM OWENS

JAFEICA Publishing
Enterprise, Alabama

Also available as an ebook for:
- Kindle
- iBooks
- Nook
- Kobo

Visit our website at:
www.jarheadtop.com

Cover image:
Staff Sgt. Joel Micholick, U.S. Army Marksmanship Unit, fires his
service rifle during the 50th Interservice Rifle Championship July
26, 2011. Micholick set a new match record in the 1,000 yard
aggregate with the service rifle, a record that had been standing
since 1984.
(Photo by Michael Molinaro, USAMU PAO, US ARMY Photo)

Print design by
LOOSE CANNON ENTERPRISES
Paradise, CA
www.loose-cannon.com

This book is dedicated to...
Terry and Daniele Haber

In the course of polite conversation, people mention my books and call me an "Author." It embarrasses me and I cover with something like "I'm quite proud of myself; I'm the first functional illiterate in my family to write a book." I have to admit it does give me a Devilish pleasure to imagine my High School English teacher turning over in his grave every time someone calls me an "Author."

It was New Years eve 1993. My wife Robbie and I were invited to a party at the home of Terry and Daniele. Anyone who can call Terry and Daniele "Friend" knows they have won the lottery; I have!!!

The youngest Grand-Baby was nice enough to share her flu with us and we were still feeling the effects, and we said our good-byes a little after midnight. On the way out the door, I had given Daniele a hard copy of the first two chapters of this book to look over. She said "Oh, I have something for you." She handed me a small white box. "What is it?" I ask. "Open it and see!" She said.

It was a desk name plate; with the simple inscription which put a lump in my throat. The incredible honor I felt at that moment washed over me, and I was at a loss for words. Before I had a chance to recover, Daniel pushed me over the edge when she said "We are so proud of you." I responded with the only way I could think of; a bear hug.

I regained my composure and still feeling that I had just been bestowed the honor of my lifetime. I went back down to the rec-room to show the gang the inscription. It read:

M/SGT JAMES R. OWENS (RET)
AUTHOR

As for my old High School English teacher Mr. Harriman, "SPIN-BABY-SPIN."

About the Cover Photograph

At the end of the DCM (Director of Civilian Marksmanship, before it was changed to CMP - "Civilian Marksmanship Program") week at Camp Perry they hold an impressive awards ceremony in the base theater. My daughter, Maria noticed that as each individual went up to get his award, the whole audience applauded, but the members of the individual's team stood. Army, Marine Corps, Air Force, Navy, and State Teams each gave their own a "standing ovation." The National Trophy Team Match is THE biggest and most prestigious match for the Service Teams. The Army had won the NTT Match. As the members of the Army team walked down to the stage, the entire Army and Marine Corps Teams stood and applauded.

My daughter asked: "Why is the entire Marine Corps Team standing and applauding?" "Respect and Sportsmanship!" I told her. Competition is fierce and the rivalry is great, but once the match is over these two professional teams give each other the respect that has been earned.

The theater was quiet as each member received his award. From two rows behind me, in a voice that filled the auditorium, a Gunnery Sergeant said "WAY TO GO, ARMY!" The applause that filled that theater was twice as loud and twice as long as any previous round. That applause was for respect and sportsmanship, not just for the Marine Corps Team, but for the shooting sport as a whole. One time a member of the AMU (Army Marksmanship Unit) liked my across the course data book, BUT, he felt he could not use it with the "Marine Corps Emblem" on the cover. So he covered it with a piece of adhesive tape. I thought it was funny. When I first saw the picture, I immediately recognized the patch on the shooters jacket as the emblem of the AMU. At first I considered not using the picture, although the picture is in the public domain (means anyone can use it) and "Once a Marine, Always a Marine."

But once again, reality "Yanked my choker chain." I always have and always will have the utmost respect and admiration for the Army Marksmanship Team. They are a great team, and great individual people. This is a great picture and I view it as a tribute and recognition to their many accomplishments.

"WAY TO GO, ARMY!"

Table of Contents

Foreword

There is nothing more confusing to the new shooter (and some old ones), than the use of the leather sling and reading the wind. I learned to shoot in Marine Corps Boot Camp, and we used the web sling. In 1965, I started shooting competitive high power, and was taught the use of the leather sling. Like every-one else, I found it rather awkward and bothersome. I was shooting sitting rapid groups that would qualify as 99 or 100's on today's targets. I asked my coach, "Can I use the web sling?" He said, "Sure," and for two days my groups opened up about four inches. I went back to the leather sling and have not touched a web sling since. Mitchell Maxberry a former National Champion has a dissenting opinion, in chapter two.

I can show you about six different ways to use the leather sling. I will show you two of these methods in Chapters One, Two and Three. If you use the method shown in Chapter One, be prepared to take some kidding from your friends. Mine call this the "backwards" method. The hooks are facing in towards the stock while in the "parade position", instead of outboard, or away from the stock.

I was taught this "backwards" method almost thirty-five years ago at the Eastern Division and Marine Corps Matches. It felt strange at first, I almost gave up on it. But, I stayed with it, and found it worked better than the other methods.

Old habits die hard. While coaching one of my students at Camp Perry, his scorekeeper said, "You have your sling on backwards." I replied, "NO, it's on different; it's not backwards."

The 1907 Leather Service Rifle Sling has four parts; a long strap, a short strap and two "keepers." I will show you the "backwards" method in Chapter Nine.

A new method has come along and has been improved upon that is even better. It is called the "No Pulse" method and I will show it to you in Chapter Ten.

The "No Pulse" method has several advantages:

1. It does not give a pulse beat from the arm which translates to (movement) of the front sight.
2. The "No Pulse" sling can be placed on the arm while waiting on the ready line without handling the rifle.
3. When you are called to the firing line, the sling can be attached to the rifle in 10 seconds or less.

CHAPTER ONE

Positions

Shooting positions have always been a tough subject for me. One reason is obvious... different people's sizes and body configurations. On a team, you may have Olive Oyl's skinny brother, who is 6'3" tall, Fat Albert's overweight (by family standards) cousin, who is 5'4" tall, and Laverne and Shirley's two boyfriends who have beer guts acquired while trying to keep Shotz's Brewery profitable.

The only way to handle these variants is to give good basic information on the different shooting positions, offering viable alternatives, and then leave it up to the individual to alter their position to suit his or her own body configuration.

There is one other thing that bothered me about teaching shooting positions. I have a flair for catching the incredibly obvious. I am pretty good at noticing the glaringly obvious. From there, I go downhill fast. When I agree to help a person with their position; if the mistakes are incredibly, or even glaringly obvious, I can quickly correct the position. Once they come within a normal range of "acceptable" position, I start to get this great feeling of inadequacy, and feel like a bump on a log. I then revert to the same old dumb saying as everyone else, "How does that feel?" The new shooter has no idea, what-so-ever, as to how it should feel. He says aloud, "OK," and under his breath, says, "I think?"

At that point, the coach usually does another incredibly dumb thing by having the new shooter mark his sling setting for that position, and tells him to use it for the rest of his life, or until the sling stretches. For twenty-seven years I used the same method as all other coaches. In my twenty-eighth year (I catch on fast), I sat down to analyze the situation, and came up with something different.

I have developed a four step theory on how the positions should "feel." This is a key to 75% of the positions you will use. I have tested my theory on my High Power Rifle Classes, and most of the people responded that it did help them.

Most people teach the positions in the order that they are shot: Off-Hand (Standing), Sitting, Prone Rapid and Prone Slow. I will cover them in a different order. The first three steps of my theory affect the Prone Rapid, Prone Slow and the Sitting positions. I present the four steps, and then the positions in that order, adding the Off-Hand at the end.

I have other theories that I will be adding. You will see that some of them fly in the face of "conventional wisdom," and are even opposite of the mainstream. I took a chance with the "Amended Grid Lines," and a lot of people said, "they work." Go ahead and try them. You can always go back to your old ways. Someday, give me a call or come up to me at Camp Perry, and tell me if they work or not.

* * *

As I mentioned, the new shooter doesn't know how the position should "feel." A position is adopted through trial and error. In this chapter, I will give you a four step process that should alleviate the confusion. The first three steps can be done at home, and the fourth must be done on the range.

How many times have you heard the statement, "The key to shooting (or positions) is consistency; you must do the same thing each and every shot!" That is true, up to a point. If you are shooting poorly or something is wrong, even for just that string of fire, by doing things consistently, you will do nothing more than shoot consistently poor.

If you know your ability is higher than the scores you are

getting, change something, even after just six or seven shots. What have you got to lose? I will give you examples of these changes throughout the book.

The Four Steps

Step One: The "Flat" of the arm.

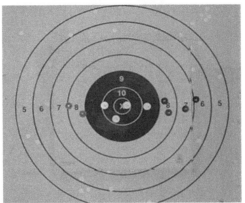

(Rapid fire group, horizontal, arm on elbow)
Fig. 1

One of the largest problems for a shooter in the prone position is that he will have his sling adjusted so that his <u>left arm is sharply bent and resting on the elbow</u>. Figure 1 shows the result of this position on a rapid fire target. The shots are spread out, horizontally. To avoid this, <u>you need the "flat" of the arm resting on the mat</u> and the arm parallel to and slightly under the rifle.

(Flat of the arm 6-8 inches above the elbow)
Fig. 2

To find the "flat" of the arm (Fig. 2): Wear a short sleeve shirt, or roll up the left sleeve to well above the elbow. Place the fingers of your left hand onto your right shoulder. Touch your left elbow with the fingers of your right hand. Now move the fingers up the back side of the arm about two or three inches.. The "flat" of the arm is that area; it is about the size of your four fingers. If you apply some pressure to this area, you will find it pretty solid. If you move further up the arm to the underside of the muscle and apply pressure—the muscle and skin will give. Identifying the "flat" of the arm is Step One.

Step Two: Get the "Feel" of the position.

Like taking a practice swing in golf, you want to get the "feel" of the position. On your living room carpet, you can lay down and get the "feel" of the prone position. <u>WITHOUT your shooting equipment (rifle, sling, jacket, etc.)</u>, lay down on the carpet with your chest flat on the floor.

Now turn slightly to your left side, about an eighth of a turn, so that you are on your rib cage and not laying flat on your chest. The latter can cause your breathing to be impaired.

If you did a full turn, you would roll completely over and end up back on your chest. A half turn and you would roll onto your back, one fourth of a turn to the left and you would be on your left side. Now you see what I meant by an eighth of a turn.

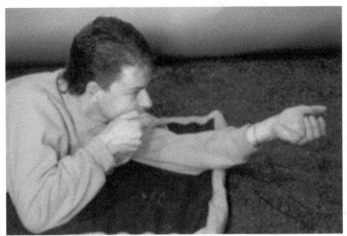

Getting the "Feel" of the position without the shooting gear
Fig. 3

Extend your **left shoulder** towards the target, this extends your whole left arm out in front of you until the "**flat**" of the arm rests on the carpet. Your left forearm will form a natural upwards angle (Fig. 3). By the way, the rules say the part of the arm below the elbow (From the elbow to the wrist) **May Not touch** the shooting mat or the ground.

Your head is raised slightly and looking at a distant object or spot on the wall. If you draw an imaginary line from that spot and your head, your left arm should be pointed just to the left of that line and parallel to it.

Now lift the left arm and move it slightly to the right (if you can), about an inch or so. This will get the left arm under the rifle and help eliminate some of the horizontal disbursement of your shots.

Place the knuckle of your right thumb just below your right cheek and rotate your right elbow down until it rests on the carpet.

The right leg drawn up
Fig. 4

Step Three: Get the position WITH your shooting gear.

Now suit up with your equipment and rifle, and do it again. First put on your sweat shirt. Always use a sweat shirt. It fills out the shooting jacket, adds padding and keeps the body temperature at a consistent (HOT) temperature. A heavy sweat shirt with a hood is best. The hood protects your neck from: other shooters' flying brass, the friction of your jacket collar, and on a cold windy day, that hood is worth it's weight in gold.

Testing for fit
Fig. 5

Put your shooting jacket on. When testing for fit of a jacket, place both elbows out in front of your body and try to touch them together (Fig. 5).

If you can touch them, you will have enough room in the jacket to get into all the shooting positions. Be sure to wear the sweat shirt when testing for fit.

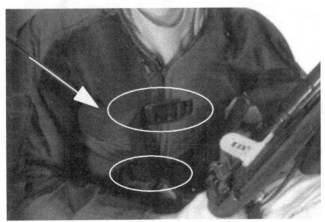

Only the top 2 buckles are used for sitting & prone
Fig. 6

17

Only the top two buckles are used for the prone and sitting positions (Fig. 6).

The rest are left open and the bottom of the coat flares out on each side. I pull the top two buckles almost as tight as they will go. You will have to work on what works for you.

Remember as you are suiting up, use all of the equipment you will be using when you shoot, except a live round. Don't forget your ear muffs! You will place your head on the stock differently with them off than you would with them on. Same goes for the glove.

Place the sling on your left arm and adjust it until it "feels" about where you were in step two. When you first put it on your arm and try to get down into position, it will be far too tight. You will have to adjust the hooks until you can get the right "feel."

The sling will have to be a little tighter than the "feel" in step two. Most people wear the sling far too tight. Remember Steve Allerman? You don't want it too loose either. Have someone take the rifle in their right hand and try to move it side to side while you are in the prone position. They should be able to move it a little, but the motion should not be sloppy.

Left hand does not grip the rifle
Fig. 7

18

The left hand: Look at the palm of your left hand. The line that runs from the center of your wrist diagonally to the left side of the base of the first finger is known as your "Life Line." The rifle will lay in your glove along this line; **your hand is relaxed, you do not grip the rifle. The fingers are relaxed and loose** (Fig. 7).

The Glove: Always wear a shooting glove on your left hand. One of the new shooters was offered the use of a glove and he said, "I'll tough it out." You might as well save your ammo—unless you are into pain.

You would be amazed at how much of the recoil is taken up by that left hand. Shoot a 300 Winchester Magnum one time and you'll get the idea. With a properly adjusted sling (shooting a .308, a 30-06 or a .223), you won't even notice the recoil taken up by the left hand. During one string of fire, I paid particular attention to it and I could tell the hand was absorbing some of the recoil.

Gehmann makes an excellent shooting glove and it is pretty popular with High Power shooters today. The old yellow glove was good in its day, and is still acceptable today. The "Mitt" used in small bore is not good for High Power, it gives a slight bounce during rapid fire.

I have more small points to cover, but I think I should save them for the section of the "Prone Position."

Once you have established a good prone position, mark your sling settings (the holes that the hooks are in), so that you can be sure to get the same setting next time you fire on the range.

In the name of consistency, some shooters refuse to change their sling setting, once it is marked. If your clothes stretched, you'd have them taken in. If the sling stretches, start over & remark it!

Step Four: "Testing" the sling for the proper setting or holes.

We were shooting a Wednesday night practice at six hundred yards. I plot my shots in my data book very accurately. I noticed my first ten shots were terrible, the group was spread and nothing was close to the center. I was so disgusted, I had to do something. I don't know why I did it, but I got out of position and changed my sling setting by one notch. I laid back down and fired the second ten shots. They all came up center, tens and X's.

I don't remember if I let the sling out a notch or if I took it up a notch (let it out, I think). The point is, I changed something. Consistency only goes so far.

Part of the problem with poor shooting (wide shots) could be nothing more than an improperly adjusted sling, even if you dry fired with it first.

CHAPTER TWO

Rule Changes

In the past few years there have been some rule changes both to NRA and CMP. Several of these changes have to do with the "loading procedure" for the 200 yard and 300 yard rapid fire strings. Yes, you guessed it, they are totally different from each other.

The major difference is **CMP has to stand up** and load prior to the rapid fire string, while **NRA cannot stand** for the rapid fire strings. Both the NRA and CMP loading procedures are totally different as well.

I will get into the details on each procedure so you will understand how each is handled for the CMP and NRA competitions. First you must understand some things about "the World of Competitive High Power Shooting."

Both CMP and NRA "Across the course shooting is based on; slow fire standing 200 yards, rapid fire sitting 200 yards, rapid fire prone 300 yards and slow fire prone 600 yards. All of these are shot at the those given distances or on reduce course targets to simulate those distances. NRA also has long-range matches, 600 yards 800 yards 900 yards and 1,000 yards (All are fired in the prone position).

CMP has its own rulebook and NRA has its own rulebook. If you were firing a CMP match you would of course fire under CMP rules. In many cases the rules for the two organizations do match. If there is something that is not covered by the CMP rule, CMP will defer to the NRA rulebook.

Now just to make your life a little more interesting, we throw "People" into the mix. Different ranges, you will find will have different <u>interpretation</u> of these rules.

Here is one of the new rules the shooters love and the range officials hate. First you need to understand the way things used to be... When the tower or "Center of the line" called a "Relay to the line" the shooters have two minutes to take their firing point. The shooter could set up his gear (scope, stool, mat etc.) but he could not handle his rifle until the start of the three minute preparation period.

When the three minute preparation period began the shooter could now pick up the rifle, place the sling on his arm and then get down into the shooting position and dry fire (No live rounds can be fired in the preparation time).

In High Power Rifle shooting there are two worlds; local ranges and Camp Perry Nationals. Most all of the local ranges will allow the shooter to set up his scope, mat and shooting stool prior to being called to the line. Camp Perry will not allow such flagrant disregard for safety, even though a scope, mat or stool has never shot anyone and most likely never will. No one listens to me.

Now comes the rule change:

<u>CMP and NRA rules now allow; when the shooter is called to the line, he may immediately (prior to the start of the preparation time) place the sling on the rifle and on his arm. He may get down into position and point the rifle down range and establish his position.</u> This gives the shooter two additional minutes to get ready. He may not insert a magazine, remove the flag safety (ECI - empty chamber indicator) or close the bolt and dry fire until the start of the three minute preparation time. The shooters love it but the range officials (At Camp Perry) hate it.

Some local ranges do not keep up with the rule changes and/or they still do things the old way (No handling the rifle until the start of prep time), "because, this is the way we have always done it."

Rapid Fire Loading Procedures – NRA

In the past shooters had to stand up, then load for rapid fire, when the target started to come up the shooter would drop down into position to fire his string of rapid fire. For a while the shooter had the option to either stand up or he could stay down in position and not have to stand for his rapid fire strings.

Under current NRA rules for sitting and prone rapid fire **the shooter MUST stay down in position. The ammunition must remain on the shooting stool or the shooting mat** and **the rifle must remain out of the shooters shoulder until the targets appear.** When the target starts to come up, the shooter picks up the magazine with ammunition, loads it into the rifle and then places the rifle into his shoulder and begins to fire.

Under NRA rules for Service Rifle's (AR-15 or M1A) the shooter has the option of loading two rounds in the first magazine and eight rounds in the second magazine or the shooter has the option of loading five rounds in the first magazine and five rounds in the second magazine.

For the M-1 Garand shooters, on the command "Stand by" the shooter may take an empty clip along with two rounds and place them in the open well, but may not close the bolt until the targets appear (Fig. 8).

Fig. 8

Rapid Fire Loading Procedures - CMP

Under current CMP rules for rapid fire sitting and prone positions **the shooter MUST stand up.** When the command "Load" is given, the **shooter will close the bolt on an empty chamber**, and **then insert the magazine into the rifle.** When the targets appear the shooter drops down into position and operates the bolt (Picking up a round from the magazine and places it into the chamber) he then places the rifle in the shoulder and begins to fire the string of fire.

Under CMP rules for Service Rifle's (AR-15 or M1A) the shooter no longer has the option of loading five rounds in the first magazine and five rounds in the second magazine. The shooter must load two rounds in the first magazine and eight rounds in the second magazine.

For the M-1 Garand shooters, two rounds are placed into the well and pushed down until the bolt overrides the two rounds and the bolt is closed onto an empty chamber. When the targets appear the shooter drops down into position and operates the bolt places, the rifle in the shoulder and begins to fire.

Two rounds and an empty clip
Fig. 9

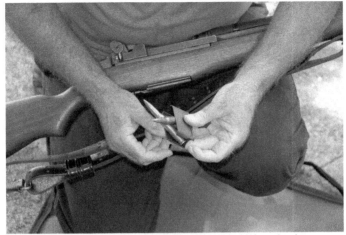

Cross the two rounds, the spring clip will hold them in place
Fig. 10

Place the two rounds and the clip in the receiver
Fig. 11

Push down on the two rounds, they will uncross
Fig. 12

Fig. 13

The next step is to override the two rounds so they will not chamber a round

With your thumb push down on the two rounds until they
are below the level of the chamber
Fig. 14

With the side of your hand, pull back on the operating rod
and slowly ride it forward
Fig. 15

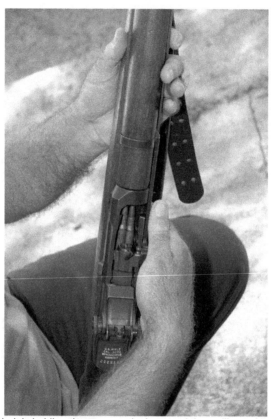

The bolt is holding the two rounds down and they will not chamber
Fig. 16

Make sure your thumb is well clear and quickly bring
your hand up and away. The operating rod spring
will close **the bolt onto the empty chamber**.
Fig. 17

When the targets appear, drop down into your shooting
position. Pull the operating rod all the way to the rear and
release it. The bolt will pick up a round and feed it into the
chamber. Place the rifle into your shoulder and you are ready
to shoot.

The "M-1 Thumb" versus the "AR Pinky"

Anyone who has ever shot an M-1 Garand is or should be well
aware of the dangers of the dreaded M-1 thumb. While closing
the bolt on the M-1 Garand if not done properly, the shooters
thumb can be slammed into the receiver by the bolt.

Usually the thumb will turn "black and blue" and in some cases the thumbnail will fall off. Ouch. This is not a case of the person being stupid, it is a case of they were not properly trained.

To close the bolt on an M-1 Garand (with or without ammunition) the shooter needs to press down on the "Follower" with his right thumb (the follower is the parts you can see when you look into the receiver) the follower pushes up on the rounds and acts pretty much as the spring does in a magazine.

While pushing down on the follower (or ammunition if used) the shooter has to at the same time, use the side of his right hand to pull back on the handle of the op-rod. This releases the catch on the left side of the receiver.

Now, if you do not want one of these M-1 thumbs, the thing to do is bring your right hand up and away from the rifle FAST. The op-rod spring will slam the bolt home, and if you "ride" the rod forward slowly, the bolt will slam home taking your thumb with it.

The AR Pinky

I coined the phrase "AR Pinky" some years ago. I have seen two cases and both times there was blood everywhere. Mostly in the receiver and the ejection port. Blood in the receiver just makes it that much harder to clean.

To close the bolt on the AR-15, the bolt release is on the left side of the receiver. The shooter will usually <u>reach over</u> the carry handle and uses his thumb to push the release and the bolt will slam forward.

The problem comes when the person <u>reaches through the carry handle instead of over it.</u> When the shooter uses his thumb and reaches under the carry handle he tends to forget the rest of the right hand curves inward, sometimes to the point of having the Pinky curve into the ejection port. Again Ouch. "Forewarned is forearmed."

CHAPTER THREE

D o you know the difference between a "Fairy Tale" and a "Marine Corps Sea story?" A Fairy Tale starts with "Once upon a time." A Marine Corps Sea Story starts with "This is No S#!T." In 1967 or 68, while I was on the Cherry Point Rifle & Pistol Team, I had a team mate, S/Sgt. Bill Goth. Bill had a Saint Bernard named "Snuffy." Snuffy wasn't a puppy nor was he full grown yet, more like a teenager. He was very friendly and extremely playful. He loved to play tug-of-war with a rag or your hat.

Snuffy had the run of the Cherry Point Range. He would turn up in places and at times you would least expect. While practicing off-hand (standing position), you would see Snuffy down by the number boards, watching the targets go up and down.

I was getting ready for the 200 yd rapid sitting; I had the sling on my arm and had just gotten into position. From behind, Snuffy had placed a paw on each of my shoulders and he let himself go limp. He just sagged down on my back. All I could do was rotate my right shoulder and say, "Snuffy, get off me."

A couple of weeks later, as I exited the range office, came around the Quonset hut, and headed toward the pistol range. The dry fire/ snapping-in range was next to the range office. As I came around the corner, I saw a Marine Lieutenant laughing. He wasn't just laughing, he was bent over, holding his sides, laughing.

His friend, another Marine Lieutenant, was in the prone position. The sling was on his left arm, stretched out it wasn't of much use to him. All he could do was rotate his right shoulder and squirm a lot. He was fruitlessly trying to dislodge a very horny Saint Bernard, who was blissfully humping away.

I had to laugh too. I went over and got hold of Snuffy's collar and disengaged him from the frustrated Lt. With Snuffy in hand, I immediately left the area, leaving the poor guy with what little dignity he could muster. Besides I sure as hell didn't want to stick around and answer any questions.

NATURAL POINT OF AIM

I'm not going to go too deeply into the natural point of aim since this was covered pretty well in my last book, "*Sight Alignment and Trigger Control.*"

I am however going to discuss the importance of keeping the feet in place for long range shooting.

I was keeping score at a 1,000 yds. match and the shooter in front of me was a lady Marine Lieutenant. Her feet were flopping around so much they reminded me of a couple of salmon after being thrown up onto the river bank by a grizzly bear.

There are four elements to the aiming process: 1) eye, 2) rear sight, 3) front sight and 4) aiming black or "Bulls Eye."

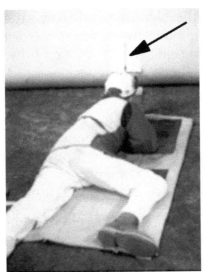

Fig. 18 Front sight is in line with rod & target

There is an experiment that demonstrates the natural point of aim and the importance of keeping one's feet still. Have the shooter get into their best prone position. His eye, rear sight, front sight and the distant aiming black will all be within the "Line of Sight." Take a long rifle cleaning rod, and stand it vertical on the ground just in front of his muzzle Fig. 18.

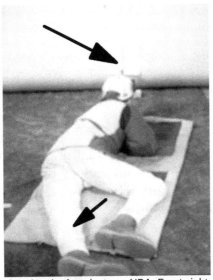

(Moving the feet destroys NPA, Front sight
moved to the left of the rod & target)
Fig. 19

He will now see the cleaning rod (Now, the fifth element) in the "Line of Sight." Have the shooter move his left foot six to eight inches to the right Fig. 19. Notice how the muzzle of his rifle shifted just to the left of the rod.

Assuming he had a natural point of aim to begin with, he no longer has a line of sight to the aiming black. This change is enough to throw his shots completely off the target. He now has to muscle the rifle with his left arm to re-align the sights. When you muscle the gun and are not using bone support you fatigue quickly and it makes shooting more difficult.

Maybe you don't move your feet six to eight inches at a time. You will get the same, but smaller, results by using a series of small moves. <u>Keep the feet in place.</u>

AN ILLEGAL PRONE POSITION

I have seen several illegal Off-Hand and a few Sitting positions. I never gave much thought to an illegal Prone Position. One time, we were shooting the first Wisconsin State Four Gun Six Hundred Yard Championship at La Crosse, WI. The gentleman to my right had a prone position I had never seen before. His score keeper and I looked at it, and each other, and shrugged our shoulders.

He wasn't shooting all that well. What made his prone position so unusual was that his left arm was entirely flat on the ground. From his shoulder to his wrist, the wrist was turned upward at almost a ninety degree angle to support the rifle.

At the Competitors' meeting at Camp Perry in 1993, some of the shooters were again complaining of the Line Officials harassing the shooters about illegal positions. More on this later. Mid Thompkins said, "Hell, you want to see harassment—shoot small bore—the line official will come up with a protractor and measure the angle of your forearm to the ground."

I got to thinking of our friend with his forearm flat on the ground. I checked the NRA High Power Rule Book. Rule 5.6 states in part, <u>"No portion of the arms below the elbows shall</u>

rest upon the ground." That makes our friend's position illegal.

INFORMING OR HARASSMENT

The National Matches at Camp Perry, OH cannot be run each year without the help of the wonderful people known as "Volunteers." They come from great distances and put in long, hard hours to make the National Matches work. They work hard and take the job seriously (most of them, anyway). For the most part, they are not shooters and after reading the rule book or listening to their briefing, some of them will get over zealous in the performance of their duties.

The competitors feel it is their (the competitor's) responsibility to police each other for illegal positions, and/or equipment (They are correct). Some volunteers feel it is their responsibility, and when they see something they feel "is not right," they ATTACK immediately. Usually this happens during the Slow Fire string of fire. This disrupts the shooters concentration; then the shooter loses concentration; and he has to defend his shooting position. His scores go downhill during the rest of the string. He becomes angrier, and hard feelings begin between the shooter and the officials. If the volunteer feels he sees something he thinks is illegal or not correct, he should call for the Referee and ask him to look at the position or equipment. That is the Referee's job, not the line officers.

Several years ago at Camp Perry, I was scoring for an Expert who was shooting Off-Hand. His position was glaringly illegal - he was using artificial support to the max. He had his ammo on his belt and he rested his left elbow on the ammo pouch. And he wasn't shooting very well, so I did not interrupt him during his string. When he finished, I said, "See that NRA referee over there? I know him pretty well, and if he had seen your Off-Hand position, he would have disqualified your score and kicked you off the line." When he asked why, I explained the artificial support, and he said, "I have been shooting for three years now, and no one has ever told me that."

Paragraph 5.6 in the High Power Rule Book says in part, "The magazine may not compress the coat to the ground so as to provide artificial support." Rule 5.4 states, "The magazine of the rifle may touch the person or clothing of the shooter, but may not touch the ground or be used to provide artificial support."

Magazine Compressing the Jacket
Fig. 20

KILLER SPIDERS

Nowadays, in NRA Competition, you can use a shooting mat and with Hawk-Eye shooting adhesive sprayed on the mat, your right arm will never slip out of place during a string of rapid fire. Use too much Hawk-Eye and you may never separate your mat from your jacket.

In Marine Corps Competition, mats or ground cloths are not allowed. After much discussion with the Match Director, he usually will allow the use of a poncho, from the waist down only. Since the upper part of the body must be on the ground, the problem of the right elbow slipping out is more prevalent.

Since Hawk-Eye adhesive doesn't seem to work too well directly on grass, and the fact that in the "old days," Hawk-Eye wasn't made yet, the Old Timers (coaches) had other means of handling the problem. Their advice was to find a "natural" hole on the firing line on your point. By placing your right elbow in this "natural" hole, it would help with the slipping problem.

"Natural" holes are sometimes hard to find. You could frequently find someone preserving his life by crushing a "Killer Spider" with the heel of his boot and spinning around a time or two to make sure it was dead. It was fun to watch the amazed look on his face when he "discovered" the natural hole left in its place! Rule 5.2 says in part, "Digging of elbow or heel holes at the firing points which form artificial support for the elbows, arms or legs, is prohibited."

If you cannot use a mat and Hawk-Eye, some other helpful things are: try adjusting the sling, pulling up the right leg, and worst case if the right elbow does slip out during the string of prone rapid, pull it back each and every time.

HOW DO YOU OPERATE THE BOLT ?

That question caught me off guard and I did not have an answer. It was like asking, "How do you breathe?" "I don't know, I just do." I had just got my handy dandy new camcorder and had someone video tape me during a string of rapid fire.

People have told me that I operate the bolt very quickly and very smoothly. The first time I saw it on tape, I impressed myself. It was so fast that I could not analyze it. I put the tape on slow motion and it was still too fast to analyze. I have the option of freeze frame and can advance the tape one frame at a time. My reaction was "WOW, is that neat!" One motion flows smoothly into the next; several things taking place simultaneously.

Finger lifting the bolt
Fig. 21

During a string of rapid fire: As the shot is fired, the fingers release the small of the stock and the right hand starts to rise. The left edge of the index finger is naturally facing up. It catches the bolt and as the hand rises, the bolt is unlocked. (Fig. 21)

Two fingers hooked on the bolt
Fig. 22

When the bolt reaches the top of its track, the wrist cocks slightly upward and the index and middle fingers hook the bolt as the hand moves to the rear. The two fingers hook the bolt near the tips of the fingers. (Fig 22)

Bolt pushed forward by base of the thumb
Fig. 23

As the bolt reaches its track to the rear, the wrist rotates and the bolt is pushed forward by the meaty pad of flesh at the base of the thumb (Fig 23).

Fig. 24 Thumb locking the bolt down

When the bolt reaches the forward part of its track, the thumb pulls the bolt down Fig 24 and locks it as the hand travels back to the small, or grip, of the stock.

It is done so quickly & smoothly, that I now know why bolt gunners like it. "You can go as fast as you want to; you don't have to wait on the gas system."

I have seen other shooters grip the bolt handle with the thumb and index finger, and operate it in the usual manner. I have seen them operate the bolt quickly and smoothly, using this manner. If it works for them - Great.

I have noticed I am developing a callus along the edge of my index finger. I got to thinking, 4,000 or 5,000 rounds per year for the past six years could be the cause of the callous starting to develop.

TAKE A WALK DOWN THE LINE

Of the ranges across the country I have fired on, nearly thirty of them follow an unwritten law. They all assign High Masters to the first relay and finish filling out the relay with Masters. It is done as a professional courtesy for one, (they have earned it), and number two, it helps the statistical (scoring) office. The match winner is probably going to come from that relay and it makes them easier to find if you keep them together. It gives the probable Match winners the same shooting conditions as their competitors.

Camp Perry is the notable exception. They spread the High Masters out so the other classifications have a chance to talk with them and possibility learns something. They do keep the high fifty shooters from the previous year together.

In Chapter Five, I will discuss the basic principles for the prone position. I'll cover them again in the next chapter, along with the sitting and off-hand in coming chapters.

Many shooters will find it interesting to walk down the ready line behind the first relay, High Masters and Masters, and take a look at their basic positions. A surprising number will have positions close to the points outlined here. The variations are interesting also. The Warrant Officer that had an off-hand position where he leaned back to the point of being ridiculous, shot some very good off-hand scores. He was outside the main stream, but it worked for him.

CHAPTER FOUR

This chapter will cover the prone (laying on your abdomen) position for long range slow fire shooting. For 600, 800, 900 and 1,000 yards slow fire and their reduced course equivalents.

A small tidbit of long-range shooting I find interesting. In the late 1800s and early 1900s 1000 yard rifle matches were quite popular. Spectators of the time lined both sides of the range similar to what golf spectators do today. They lined both sides of the range from the target to the shooters on the firing line.

Most of the shooters used the "Kentucky Long Rifle." They did not use the prone position as we use today. The shooter would lay on his back, his feet pointing toward the targets down range. The shooter would then place the long barrel of the rifle between his feet, and then raise his head to aim the sights. That position came to be known as the "Creedmoor" position.

The Prone Position

The rule book simply describes the prone position as: *"Body extended on the ground, head toward the target. The rifle will be supported by both hands and one shoulder only. **No portion of the arms below the elbows** shall rest upon the ground or any artificial support, nor may any portion of the rifle rest against any artificial support."*

I will outline the basic prone position I use. Once again the key parts are:

Lay down with your head toward the target, flat on your chest;

now turn slightly to your left side. This gets the pressure off the lungs and this keeps your breathing from being impaired.

The forearm forms an upward angle
Fig. 25

Extend your **left shoulder** towards the target, this extends your entire left arm out in front of you until the **"flat"** of the arm rests on the shooting mat. Your left forearm will form a natural upwards angle (Fig. 25). By the way, the rules say the part of the arm below the elbow (From the elbow to the wrist) **May Not touch** the shooting mat or the ground.

Shift length of body around until you reach your natural point of aim (The distant target, front sight, rear sight, your eyes, all in one line).

The body is "Behind" the rifle and the right leg is drawn up

Fig. 26

Your right shoulder and the Length of your body is behind the rifle Fig 26. The right leg should be drawn up about one-third the way, this keeps the pressure off the lungs, abdomen, beer gut, etc.

The spotting scope is set so the shooter only has to move his head slightly to the side to be able to effectively see his target. Having the scope too far away forces the shooter to move his body out of alignment and destroys his natural point of aim. The left leg remains in place, movement destroys natural point of aim.

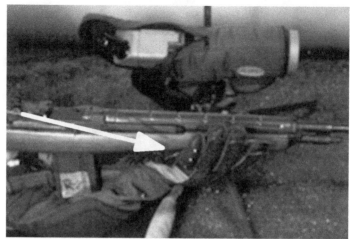

Hand does not "Grip" the stock
Fig. 27

The left hand is relaxed. Let it lay across the glove or hand, It
does not "grip" the rifle (Fig. 27).

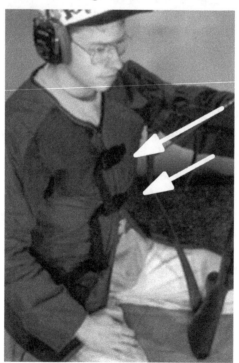

Top two buckles are used
Fig. 28

In the <u>prone and sitting positions, only the top two straps are buckled</u>, this allows greater movement while getting into position. In the Off-Hand (Standing) position <u>ALL</u> the buckles are used, this gives greater support for that position.

SLOW FIRE PRONE

Slow Fire and Rapid Fire each have different sequence, or flow. They have much in common but they have obvious and minor differences.

You are at a match and getting ready for your Slow Fire Prone. Here is where it all comes together. The basic prone position, sight alignment, trigger control, breathing, relaxation, grip, natural point of aim, safety, listening for range commands, reading the wind, watching for wind change, and a dozen other small things to make your life miserable while you are having fun.

Socialize and have fun, BUT, use your time wisely. Before the tower calls you to the line, make sure certain things are taken care of. Make sure you have the correct elevation and windage on your rifle. You look and feel pretty silly if you still have your three hundred yard Rapid fire zero on the rifle, and you are shooting six hundred yard Slow fire.

Fill out your data book as much as you can. 75 - 80% can be filled in before going to the line, such as; the date, the range you are on, your target number, your relay, the time of day, the ammo you are using, your rifle number, your sight picture your starting elevation and windage. Don't waste prep (Preparation) time on things that could have been handled earlier.

Make sure your ammo is ready and in the right amount, Again, you will look and feel silly if you left your ammo in the car, or at home, or you have the wrong ammo for that stage of fire.

Make sure your collateral equipment is ready. Timer, I like the digital one that counts down or up. At a glance, you know exactly how much time remains. If you didn't set your timer and you think you are running out of time, you will rush your shots (Range Officials are not allowed to tell you how much time is remaining, <u>Unless you ask</u>). Having a sweat band for hot days is a good idea, stinging eyes make it difficult to focus.

Have a towel, used for covering ammo from the sun (Some powders are very sensitive to heat changes). It's also good for getting a grip on a hard to turn windage knob (M1A or M-1 Garand), and mopping your brow after you discover you lost the sweat band.

Make sure you have your shooting glasses, ear muffs, data book, pens, pencils, wind charts and Saint Bernard repellent. Just seeing if you were paying attention.

If you are shooting a Service Rifle, blacken your sights. If you are shooting a Match Rifle, make sure the diopter, if you have one, is clean.

When the rifle comes out of the case, make sure the flag safety is in, the bolt is open, the safety is on, the magazine is removed, and the muzzle is pointed down range when laying on the stool.

When people are moving to or from the pits, your rifle can be in only one of two places: (1) in the gun case; or, (2) laying on the stool as described above. DO NOT HANDLE THE RIFLE WHILE PEOPLE ARE DOWN RANGE !!! If it is lying on the stool, you can blacken your sights, adjust your elevation and windage, and, even sit down behind the rifle and look through the sights, making sure you do not <u>handle the rifle</u> (Pick up the rifle while people are down range). Keep all safety features in place.

Most ranges will allow you to move some of your gear to the line early if your firing point is open. Camp Perry does not allow this - they have thousands of shooters and the tower has to control 150 firing points. They will allow gear <u>only</u> when called to the line.

The ranges that do allow gear ahead of time are pretty lenient, except for the rifle. It must remain in the case or on the stool. Allowing the gear ahead of time is perfectly acceptable (a shooting mat or scope has never shot anyone . . . yet), and it helps the shooters, they are less rushed during Prep Time.

Set up your mat first, place it on the most level piece of ground you can find and to the right of your number stake (The number stake is the same as your target number). Make sure the mat is up to the firing line and even with the number stakes. Too far back and you are going to hit the people on either side of you with a muzzle blast. Too far forward, and you are going to get hit with their muzzle blast.

After the mat, the spotting scope should be set up. The set up of the spotting scope is very important. Improperly set up, it can destroy your prone position. (Commercial time) I sell an excellent ADJUSTABLE scope stand (See my web site www.JarHeadTop.com).

Set the stand forward and to the left of the mat. Make sure the legs are adjusted so they are not under or touching your left arm. The Rambo Line Officer from Hell will disqualify you for artificial support. You think I'm kidding about *the Rambo Line Officer from Hell*? He once disqualified Gy/Sgt. Donald Hymann for having a battery-powered fan next to him on the firing line, "Changing the conditions of the Match!" Find that one in the rule book.

Scope set for minimum head movement
Fig.29

The stand should be adjusted so the eye piece is level with your eye while you are in the prone position. It should take no more movement than moving your head a few inches to look through the spotting scope.

 If you have to raise or lower your head, you do not have it set to the proper height. You should not have to roll your body to look through the scope. Your head should move four to six inches. Once again, take a walk down the firing line and watch the first relay.

STUDY THE WIND

You have your rifle, ammo, equipment, mat and scope set up and ready. There is still a little time before they call you to the line. Use this time to study the wind. Get out your wind charts; Description of natural effects and your wind charts for this yard line. Do the three steps: Estimate the speed, direction and value. This is your initial estimate, keep it in mind. Now watch for the "constant." **The "constant" is the period of time the wind stays stable or steady for the longest period of time.** The wind could blow from one direction and stay at a steady speed for a minute or two, then pick up speed (gust), then drop back to its constant. It could stay constant for a period of time then let off or die, and then pick back up to its constant.

The wind could change directions for a short period of time then return to its constant (fish tailing). Using this time prior to going to the line will save you valuable shooting time. Trying to figure the wind during your prep time, or during your shooting time, puts you behind the curve. Doing it ahead of time puts you ahead of the curve and the other shooters.

They call your relay to the line

When they call your relay to the line, they usually give the shooters a minute or two to claim their firing point before beginning the three minute prep time. Usually when the last person takes his spot, plus about twenty to thirty seconds is when they call the beginning of the three minute prep time. That is if they have the pits organized and they get the targets in the air. That last person to the line is usually the one who hasn't done any of the pre-work for preparation.

During this minute or two, you can leisurely put on your shooting jacket, leather sling and shooting glove. When the line officer says, "Your three minute prep time starts now," make sure you start your timer for the three minutes. This will give you an idea where you stand for time. More than once a line officer called the start of prep time, started talking to someone and didn't notice when the three minutes were up. I have seen four, five and six minute prep times.

I personally hate three minute prep times. They are cruel and unusual punishment. I have my stuff ready ahead of time; it only takes thirty seconds or less to throw on the jacket, sling and glove. Once I have my position and I am ready, again, another thirty seconds. I want to start. Laying down there gets me hyper. I will wait until we are two and half minutes into prep time before I lay down. That's me; I don't recommend it for other people.

"Your prep time has begun"

The start of your prep time has begun. You have your jacket, sling and glove on, you lay down and get into your position. Remember, NO sighters are to be fired during prep time. Follow all the key points and steps, make sure you are within the proper range of the spotting scope, head movement only. Move your ammo to within easy reach. Slightly forward and to your right. If it is a hot day, protect the ammo from the direct rays of the sun and heat with the towel (A white towel doesn't absorb the sun's heat a quickly and keeps your ammo at an ambient temperature). Set up the data book and clip board just in front of the ammo along with the pen or pencil. I have mine just forward of my right elbow, just close enough to not have it interfere with the position, but still plenty close.

Sometimes I find there is slight slope forward of the left elbow. The "flat" of the arm is on the mat, but nothing feels right. I push forward with the whole body and the arm shifts and "LOCKS" in place.

CHECK YOUR NUMBER BOARD

When it comes to shooting on the wrong target, there is an old saying, "THOSE WHO HAVE, THOSE WHO WILL, AND THOSE WHO WILL AGAIN." Shooting two targets away at six hundred yards during a "Leg" match, costing you a medal will make you determined to not be in the class of "Those who will again." In fact, it makes you down right paranoid.

When you take your position, check your number board and make sure your natural point of aim is on your <u>own</u> target. Check it and adjust it, and check it again. Even with a good natural point of aim, you can almost go into a trance as you shoot a string of Slow Fire. You quit paying attention to the numbers on the board and you start noticing the background color - white, black or yellow. When that happens, it is very easy to come down on a target that is two targets away from your own. More than once a little voice in my head has said, "Something is wrong," and I saved myself some embarrassment by listening and checking my number board.

The longer the distance, or range, the easier it is to crossfire. Shooting two targets away at two hundred yards is not unheard of. When you stand on the firing line and face down range to the number boards and the target, there will be a "feel" that things are "naturally" lined up. On some ranges, that "feeling" is not there. It seems everything is off to one side. That is when you really must pay attention. Another common problem is the target is off to the left or right of the number board. On some ranges, it is between the number boards. You may have to, ask a range official which is your target.

Vaile Range at Camp Perry has one hundred and fifty firing points. It is very easy to be TEN targets off, especially at long range. I know one guy who cross-fired ten targets from the two hundred yard line on that range.

If you are shooting a Match Rifle, use this prep time to make sure your front aperture is two or two and a half times the size of the aiming black (for full details see my free chapters from *Sight Alignment and Trigger Control* on my web site www.jarheadtop.com). Check the proper opening on the rear sight aperture, close it down all the way and slowly open it until a flood of light comes in, then stop. Check it to see if the polarizing filters where left on from the last time, and if they are needed this time.

At some point during your prep time, when you feel comfortable with your initial estimate of the wind, or you used a Scientific Wild Ass Guess, place the number of clicks on the rifle and remember where you are.

"YOUR PREP TIME HAS ENDED"

When you hear the line official call the end of prep time, immediately reset your timer for the twenty-two minutes Slow Fire. When he says, "With one round, load," go ahead and place one round in the chamber, but do not close the bolt. When he says, "You may commence fire, your time starts now," punch the button on your timer and set it up next to the leg on your shooting stool. Have it facing you so all you have to do is glance over. You don't want to have to go looking for it later. You don't want to have to break your position to find it.

SHOOTING THE STRING

I generally let a few other people break the first shots, especially if I'm down on one end of the line; just to the make sure the command to fire has been given.

You are now going to start your sequence and get into a routine. This sequence is repeated for each and every shot.

1. Get on the scope and check the wind. Make sure it is where you want it . . . **in the constant.** Check the range flags.
2. Make your decision. Do you need a sight adjustment?
3. Close the bolt. On the M1A and M-1 Garand, this gets the bolt handle out of the way of the windage knob. Closing the round

just before you shoot, keeps the round from sitting in a hot chamber for any great length of time (Allowing ammo to sit in a hot chamber changes the ballistics of the shot).

4. Make the sight correction. If you are not REALLY familiar with the rifle and its sights, <u>LOOK at the knob and arrow</u> as you turn the sights. Turning the sights in the wrong direction can compound your problems.

5. Take a last glance at the wind and/or range flags. They can fishtail faster than it takes to say so.

6. Place the butt of the rifle in your shoulder. The same place each time.

7. Bring the sights down to the NUMBER BOARD first. Check your number board with **each and every shot.**

8. Breathe. Take in a full breath and let it out. Take up a full breath and let it out to the point the front sight blade comes to your aiming point (Center or 6 o'clock hold).

9. Let your position take over; relax into your natural point of aim.

10. Pick up your sight alignment and sight picture.

11. **Focus your vision on the front sight post.**

12. The Slack was taken up sometime earlier. NOW squeeze the trigger. DO NOT LAY ON THE GUN. This should be done at the same cadence as Rapid Fire. Lying on the gun and trying to "Touch Up" will burn the image into your mind. The longer you lay there, the more you will misalign the sights, and the more time the wind has to make changes.

13. Call your shot. Predict where the hit will be on the target based on the way you saw your sights when the rifle fired. I can call my shots Off-Hand and pretty well in Rapid Fire. I CAN NOT call my shots Slow Fire Prone. If it didn't look good, I would not have shot it; they all look good.

14. Move your head only, look through the scope and read the wind. Call your shot based on that reading. If the wind has been coming from the left and has picked up while you are shooting, you can predict the shot will be out the right side of the ten ring. If the wind had let up while you are shooting, the shot will be out the left side. Knowing this will save you unnecessary sight changes by, "Chasing your spotter."

15. While you are checking the wind in your scope, make sure your target goes down for a mark. Scenario: You check the wind and look away before the target goes down; you start the rest of your routine. You look up, the scoring disk and the spotter are in

54

the same place as last time. You ask the score keeper, "Did he mark the target?" He says, "I don't know, I don't think so." If you call for a mark. The shot is near the last one. The pit puller hears the call for a mark, pulls the target again, and this time there is no hit. You now get what used to be called, "Maggie's Drawers." A MISS !! Scene ends! It is worth those couple of seconds to see that the target starts to go down.

16. Pick up the next round and place it into the well, but do not close the bolt.

17. Pick up the pen and call your shot in the data book - if you can.

18. Go back on the scope and wait for the target to come up. While you are waiting, keep an eye on the wind.

19. When the target comes up, check the value disk in relation to the spotter. If the spotter is obviously in the ten ring and it is disked a nine, you do not have to waste time calling for a re-disk if you and your score keeper agree. If he does not agree, then call for a re-disk, not a mark (Remember the miss?) If it still comes up the same, you may then challenge. You put up a dollar or two, depending on the program (three dollars at Camp Perry); if you win your challenge, you get your money back. If you lose . . . it goes to the "Range Officers Retirement Fund."

20. If everything was all right, quickly plot the shot in your book. Plotting it now rather than the "shot behind" method gives you two advantages: first, you plot the shot more accurately than you would in the "shot behind" method. A shot that is a wide nine becomes a nine just off the ten line in the "shot behind" method. Second, and more important, while you are plotting your shot, you can listen for your score keeper to call out the value of your last shot. Make sure you can hear him, and that the shot value is correct. You can correct a mistake now far more easily than trying later. This insures he is staying awake and paying attention. If he asks if you want him to call out the value of the shots, and you say, "NO," you lose all rights to challenge the score later.

21. Check the wind.

22. Close the bolt.

23. Make your decision and make any sight adjustments as needed.

Well, that's about it. The sequence continues in pretty much the same order. If there is a major change in the wind, you will have to put every thing on hold until you determine what you are going to do—wait it out, or move the sights.

A good string of fire usually takes me 12 - 14 minutes for the twenty-two rounds and most of that time is spent looking through the spotting scope, and watching the wind. I said it was fired at a rapid fire pace, Check your number board, breathe and come to your aiming point, **AS SOON AS YOU FOCUS ON THE FRONT SIGHT POST, SQUEEZE THE TRIGGER STRAIGHT TO THE REAR UNTIL THE HAMMER FALLS AND THE SHOT IS FIRED. DON'T LAY ON THE GUN !!**.

CHAPTER FIVE

They say, "Timing is everything." That's true in life, comedy and shooting. I have heard a friend, Uncle Bob, tell new shooters many times, "You shot that string of Rapid Fire way too fast. You had ten seconds left. Slow down and use every second for aiming. Slow down even to the point of saving a round and make sure the others are in there."

Bob's instructions got me thinking, "What do I believe about the timing of Rapid Fire?" I'm the kind of person who can hold two opposing viewpoints, and still believe both are correct. The only saving grace in this case (shooting) is one of my opinions holds for the Service Rifle and the other, and opposite opinion, holds for the Match Rifle.

SERVICE RIFLE

I learned competitive shooting with the Service Rifle, M-14. Back in the "Old Days', the rules were: for two hundred yard Sitting Rapid, you had 50 seconds; today it is 60 seconds; and, for three hundred yard Prone Rapid, you had 60 seconds, today it is 70 seconds.

The 50/60 second rule was for the Service Rifles. If you went to a match and there was one bolt gun on your relay, you got the extra ten seconds. You had to practice for the 50/60 seconds because you could not be sure there would be a bolt gun there. In Marine Corps competition there were no bolt guns so you knew you would only have the 50/60 seconds to fire your Rapid Fire strings.

Shooting Rapid Fire at those faster times forces you to develop a <u>good cadence</u>. When the sights are lined up and you are focused, squeeze off the shot and get right back on target and do it again. Don't waste time trying to touch up.

We fired our string of fire even faster than the normal 50 seconds for Sitting. In that 50 seconds we went from standing to sitting, firing our first two shots, reloaded from the belt, scoped the two shots, made a sight change, fired the eight rounds and still had time to jump back on the scope to check the group. You have to have a **GOOD CADENCE** to do all of that.

That good cadence saved my butt at the 1980 Western Division Matches. It was the second day of competition. The Marine Corps "Leg" matches are fired in two days. Twenty rounds Off-hand, ten rounds Sitting Rapid, ten rounds Prone Rapid, and twenty rounds six hundred yards Slow Fire each day. They would then add the two scores and the top ten percent of the non-distinguished shooters received "Leg" medals.

The command "Load" had been given for the three hundred yard Rapid Fire stage (Standing to prone in a time of 70 seconds). I placed the magazine in the magazine well, but I did not "lock" it fully into place. I closed the bolt (in those days you closed the bolt for rapid while still standing), it picked up the first round. When the commands were complete and the targets came up, I dropped down into the prone position and fired the first round. When I aimed and squeezed the trigger on the second round, all I heard was "click."

The magazine was not "locked" fully into place. The bolt had picked up the first round, but when I dropped down, the magazine had started to slip out of the magazine well. The front end of the magazine held pretty well with mere friction. The back end however, started to tilt down and away from the bolt. The bolt could not pick up the second round; it over rode. When the first round was fired the vibration caused the magazine to tilt a little more. Now the magazine was only held in the well by the friction on the front end and was tilted at about a thirty degree angle. . . useless.

When I heard the loud "click", I thought I had a mechanical

malfunction alibi or a bad round. I raised my arm for the alibi and waited for a line official. After what seemed a week of waiting, I saw the armorer coming towards me. I looked down and saw the magazine hanging at that awful angle and a vision flashed through my mind.

The vision was of the armorer seeing the magazine hanging there, reaching down and pulling the magazine out, and loudly announcing, "NO ALIBI."

An ocean of adrenaline must have flowed into my body. "I" ceased to function; "I" stepped back and watched, in slow motion, the incredible speed of the last ten to fifteen seconds of that string. I snapped the magazine into place, "locking" it into position, and fired the second round. The magazine change could not have taken more than two seconds. That second magazine with eight rounds was fired so fast that my conscious mind could not have controlled the shots; it was on "auto pilot overdrive." The rest of the firing line had long since quit firing. As the last shot went down range, the targets came out of the air.

My heart was pounding and I had a case of tunnel vision, the entire world disappeared. I remember absolutely nothing except the targets coming up for score and I had dropped only TWO POINTS! I finally awoke while I walked to the six hundred yard line, where I realized my heart was still pounding and I was still wearing my cartridge belt. I never wore it more than a minute or two after a rapid fire string.

That day I took a Silver medal towards Distinguished at that match. The years of training at a <u>fast cadence</u> had paid off.

BOLT GUN

I tell people that my timing with the bolt gun is so very close to the seventy seconds, on the three hundred rapid, that as the last bullet is going through the cardboard, the pit puller is pulling the target down; it tips the back end of the bullet off it's axis.

At the beginning of the season, I usually save a round because my timing is off. I then speed up a little and I'm OK for the rest of the season. I have had such a problem that I've developed a little trick to help me during the rapid fire string, especially prone rapid.

I use the timer that counts down. I set it for seventy-one seconds. When the targets start to move, I punch the start button. I know it will take at least that one second, and usually two, for all the targets to come up, and the "time" to begin. When I go down into position (CMP Rules), and as I lay the "flat" of the left arm into place, I put the timer near the left elbow, about six to eight inches to the right of it. After I've fired the first five shots, and as I am reloading, I glance at the timer. If I have 35 seconds left, I know I am right on time for me. If it is down to 30 seconds remaining, I know I took too much time in the first five shots.

When operating the bolt, be sure to count each shot. It is embarrassing to have fired five shots and waste time aiming and squeezing the trigger on an empty chamber. After the reload, and the time check, I continue to count. The first four shots are done as normal. As I operate the bolt to chamber the last round, I glance down and check the time.

I have a tendency to rush my final shot, and usually that's the one shot I drop. By checking the time on that last shot, I know where I stand. If I'm on time, I should have 7 - 8 seconds remaining, I know I can take my time and make it good. If I am down to 3 -4 seconds remaining, I know I better speed up because I have already taken up too much time. Placing the timer near my left elbow has helped me quite a bit.

SCARED BOLT GUNNER

I tell people that for speed, the Service Rifle has nothing on a seasoned Bolt Gunner. A couple of years ago at the State Championship, the Three Hundred Yard Rapid Fire Stage, I had fired my first three rounds, and on the fourth, I heard a loud "click", and nothing happened. Did I short stroke? Was it a bad round? Do I call for an alibi? I HATE re-fires, so I opened the bolt and a round went flying out. I went into overdrive auto pilot again.

I reloaded, and fired the next five rounds very, very fast, I still can not believe it. I glanced at the timer, 12 seconds remaining, NO SWEAT. I picked up an extra round from the box, loaded it, and fired it off with plenty of time left.

When the targets came up for score, I had dropped only one point; the pit puller said it was one of the first three shots. Those are the ones fired before I kicked into overdrive. The round that went flying out, had an enlarged primer pocket; and the primer fell out.

During the super fast operation of the bolt, and shooting of the second five rounds, again adrenaline kicked in and the body went on auto pilot. As an outside observer, the mind saw all this happening in slow motion as my hand was going faster than ever before. The mind says, "WOW, is that neat!" A Service Rifle can not keep up with a scared bolt gunner. Once again proving, "With the bolt gun, you can shoot as fast as you want to; you don't have to wait on the gas system."

* * *

One time, I lost my timer and that make me a very scared bolt gunner. At the next rifle match, I noticed that not only was I the first person on the line to fire a shot, I had operated the bolt and was about to break my second round as the rest of the line was firing their first round. I also noticed that I had finished shooting before the Service Rifles and I had enough time to scope my group. Scoping my group with a bolt gun is something I could not imagine until recently. After having shot a score of 100-7X, and then backed up with a 100-6X to win the 300 yard rapid fire match, I have re-evaluated my thoughts on the subject. If it looks good, shoot it. Lying on the gun and trying to make each shot perfect only leads to trouble. Don't get me wrong, you have to do ALL the steps correctly and in the proper sequence. Once again, a good cadence is worth its weight in gold.

CHAPTER SIX

300 Yd Rapid Fire Prone Position

This chapter is on the Three Hundred Yard Rapid Prone. Just about everything in the previous five chapters applies to the Rapid Fire Prone position, and I cannot repeat everything here. I will highlight some of the earlier information, concentrating on the differences and give you additional information.

Moving Back to the 300 Yard Line

As soon as you reach the three hundred yard line and set your gear down, your real, though unofficial, preparation period begins. Many people use this time foolishly, either by socializing, or checking out how their buddy shot, he's more than happy to tell you in explicit and lengthy detail.

There is nothing wrong with socializing. In fact, it is a big part of the sport. But first, take care of your preparations both physically and your mental preparation. If you wait until the three minute prep time, you will be rushed.

When loading your magazines, or stripper clips. pay attention to the number of rounds in each magazine. A shooter loaded two rounds in one magazine, and NINE rounds in the other. He was disqualified when he shot eleven rounds.

Make sure you have the correct ammunition. Several years ago, a former State Champion went to load his stripper clips for Three Rapid, and discovered he had only Slow Fire ammunition. It was set to a longer setting depth and would not feed into the magazine well for Rapid Fire. No one on the line had a bullet seater with them, but someone did have a flat file. He filed down the hollow points enough to fit the well. His score was 100 – 7X.

Round not fully seated in magazine
Fig. 30

When loading the M-14 magazine, or the M-1 Garand clip, watch out for the round that is not fully seated to the back of the magazine or clip (Fig. 30). The tip will extend over the edge of the magazine, or in case of the M1 Garand clip, one round will be taller than the others. In both cases, they will not feed correctly. You will have saved rounds, and no alibi.

With the M1 Garand clip, hold it up and sight down the tips to make sure one or more are not taller than the others. With the magazine, check to see if one of the tips is hanging over the front lip of the magazine. I have seen people take an eight round clip and bang the tips on the sole of their boots (or other objects) to seat the rounds. I could always see that one in a million chance of a grain of sand being in the wrong place, at the wrong time, giving him the proverbial hot foot.

Other things to do during this period are: fill out your data book; blacken your sights; make sure you have the correct set of holes on your sling setting (I like mine one notch tighter for Prone Rapid than for Prone Slow); make sure you have extra ammunition in case of an alibi; make sure all of your equipment is handy and at the ready. If they allow it, go ahead and set up your mat and spotting scope (Remember - NO rifles allowed on the line.)

Spend some time studying the wind. During a string of Rapid Fire, you can't be making wind changes between shots. You have to know what the wind is doing and pay attention right up to the time you drop down into position. Since you fire double strings of Rapid Fire (NRA only), and particularly at Camp Perry, it can take a long time between strings. The wind can do one hell of a change by the time you fire that second string. For the NRA matches that do fire back to back or double strings of rapid fire you do not have to put the flag safety into the rifle between strings.

In August of 1992, my "*Wind*" book came out just before Camp Perry, and the sales were going pretty well. A hand full of people were talking to me about the book on the three hundred yard line. I had just fired my first string and after the usual long wait, the wind was doing a lot of switching. As I stood there, I could feel about five or six people watching me. "Well, the guy wrote a book on the wind, what's he going to do?" Just as we were about to go down into position, I put a minute and a half on, and I came up with a 99. Talk about pressure, but I got lucky that time. I'm not going to tell you about all the times I missed the changes.

"The First Relay to the Line"

<u>CMP and NRA rules now allow; when the shooter is called to the line, he may immediately (prior to the start of the preparation time) place the sling on the rifle and on his arm. He may get down into position and point the rifle down range and establish his position.</u>

When they call your relay to the line, that is the time to put on your shooting jacket, sling and glove.

"Your Three Minute Prep Time Has Started"

65

Get your good prone position, paying attention to the basic position outlined in previous chapters. A few other things to watch for are: a little Hawk Eye on the shooting mat will help to keep your right elbow from slipping out during the string of Rapid Fire.

A special note:

NRA matches will "generally" give two Sighter shots. The Sighter shots help the shooter confirm his zero (windage and elevation) but these shots do not count for record.

CMP matches "generally" do not give Sighter shots, particularly in "LEG" Matches. Some of the CMP games will give Sighter shots.

A "major" differences for CMP and NRA rapid fire stages are; (1) CMP must stand up and NRA must stay down and (2) the loading procedure for each are different.

For the 300 yard prone rapid fire, explaining the NRA method is easier since is basically the same as slow fire prone (just shot faster).

Remember FOCUS on the Front Sight Blade
Fig. 31

"Your Three Minute Prep Time Has Ended"

NRA - If the two sighters are given, you will have a two minute time limit to fire your two sighter shots. The line will give the command "with one round, LOAD." When the targets appear your two minute time period starts.

NRA - 300 Yard Prone Rapid Fire, Ten shots in a time Limit of 70 Seconds

Under current NRA rules for sitting and prone rapid fire the shooter <u>MUST stay down in position</u>. The <u>ammunition must remain on the shooting stool or the shooting mat</u> and the <u>rifle must remain out of the shooters shoulder until the targets appear</u>. When the target starts to come up, the shooter picks up the magazine with ammunition, loads it into the rifle and then places the rifle into his shoulder and begins to fire.

Also under NRA <u>rules for Service Rifle's</u> (AR-15 or M1A) the shooter has the option of loading two rounds in the first magazine and eight rounds in the second magazine or the shooter has the option of loading five rounds in the first magazine and five rounds in the second magazine.

For the M-1 Garand shooters, on the command "Stand by" the shooter may take an empty clip along with two rounds and place them in the open well, but may not close the bolt until the targets appear (See chapter four).

When feeding a stripper clip into a bolt gun, watch where you place your thumb on the round. Too far back and the rounds will tip up and not feed; too far forward, they will jam down into the well. I have found it best to place the thumb mid way from the head or back of the bullet, to the shoulder, or neck. Push straight down and take a second to do it right; it will save thirty seconds trying to clear a jam.

From the time you were called to the line, had your three minute prep period and fired your sighters, you should by now have a good prone position. You don't even have to stand up for your rapid fire string. When the target appears simply pick up your 1st magazine, load it and close the bolt. Now you may place the rifle into your shoulder and begin to fire.

Rapid Fire Loading Procedures - CMP

Under current CMP rules for rapid fire sitting and prone positions **the shooter MUST stand up**. When the command "Load" is given, **the shooter will close the bolt on an empty chamber**, and **then insert the magazine into the rifle**. When the targets appear the shooter drops down into position and operates the bolt (Picking up a round from the magazine and places it into the chamber) he then places the rifle in the shoulder and begins to fire the string of fire.

Also under CMP rules for Service Rifle's (AR-15 or M1A) the shooter no longer has the option of loading five rounds in the first magazine and five rounds in the second magazine. The shooter must load two rounds in the first magazine and eight rounds in the second magazine.

For the M-1 Garand shooters, a clip and two rounds are placed into the well and pushed down until **the bolt overrides the two rounds** and the bolt is closed onto an empty chamber. When the targets appear the shooter drops down into position and operates the bolt, places the rifle in the shoulder and begins to fire.

During Slow Fire Prone, once you are down, you stay down. In the Rapid Fire stage (CMP), after you get your position during prep time, you have to stand up and then come back down to the same spot, or position. A couple of things will help you do this: (1) mark your position (with a piece of empty brass near your left elbow), and (2) keep your left foot in place as you stand.

MARKING YOUR POSITION

I mark my prone position by placing an empty piece of brass or other object just to the left of my left elbow, actually, the "flat" of the arm. I then know where to place the arm as I come back down into position.

"Your Prep Time Has Ended Shooters, Stand"

Now is the time to stand up, making sure you take your ammunition and your timer with you. I place both my timer and the stripper clip between the fingers of my left hand.

There is a knack to standing up and keeping your left foot in place.

Pull your right hand back close to your chest.

Lift your chest a few inches as you pull your left elbow back close to your body.

Lift your left arm off the ground and put all your weight on your right arm.

Shift your weight back so the center of gravity is over your legs, and pull your right arm up.

You should now be sitting back on your heels.

Shift your weight slightly to the left and bring your right foot forward until it is even with your left knee.

With your right hand on your right knee, lift your left knee and push yourself to a standing position.

Your right foot is slightly forward, simply pull it back until you are in a normal standing position.

You have just stood up and kept your left foot in place. Your chances of coming back to the same prone position are now far greater. Practice this at home.

"With the Bolt Closed on an Empty Chamber, LOAD"

The command "load" has been given, close the bolt on an empty chamber and insert your magazine. Make sure: (1) you have the right magazine; loading the eight round mag. first and reloading the two round mag. is not only embarrassing, it is grounds for disqualification; (2) make sure the magazine is "locked" into place.

If you have trouble loading and you hear the command, "Is the line ready?", raise your hand and yell "NO". Your score keeper should do the same. If it is a small match, they will hold up and give you a little extra time. If it is a large match, they will call, "Shoot him on the alibi relay!", and they will continue with the commands.

I explained earlier how to load the M-1 Garand, and to keep your thumb out of the way. The M-14 is simply a matter of pulling back on the bolt handle, releasing the magazine catch, and letting the op-rod go home (remember, only after you are down in position).

After you have loaded your rifle, give the wind one last check. Look at the range flags, string, bandoleer, tossed grass, etc. This is your last chance. Don't get caught in a wind change.

"IS THE LINE READY?" (3 seconds of silence)
"THE LINE IS READY." (3 seconds of silence)
"READY ON THE RIGHT." (3 seconds of silence)
"READY ON THE LEFT." (3 seconds of silence)
"READY ON THE FIRING LINE." (3 seconds of silence)

These are the proper commands and are the only ones that should be used. I cringe when I hear extra commands given during a Rapid Fire string, "You may commence firing when your target appears" is not a proper command. "Ready (not "All Ready") on the firing line", is the last command for both the shooters and the Pit Officer.

It is interesting to watch a line as the commands are being given. An <u>inexperienced</u> shooter will: stare down range at the targets; crouch down low to the ground to get a second jump on the time; get his adrenaline flowing and his heart rate up. An <u>experienced</u> shooter will: stand erect and relaxed; he will watch the green grass to help him relax, while he is listening to the commands; when he hears the last command, "Ready on the firing line", he then looks down range at the targets. He knows that <u>any target that moves is his signal to go down into position</u>. He does not have to wait on his own target. He knows that the targets will move within a 3 - 5 seconds after the last command. He knows that the time can not start until the <u>last target is all the way in the air</u>, and the full time must elapse before the first target can be withdrawn. He knows that a typical range will run one to one and half seconds over the 60 or 70 second time limit.

A target has moved and that is your signal to go down into position. Your timer is set one second more than the time limit, it will take at least that long to get all the targets up. Make sure you hit the start button when that first target moves.

Getting back to the same position is a lot simpler than getting up.

Bend your knees slightly forward and shift your weight forward.

Lower your body down to both knees.

Turn your right shoulder slightly forward and extend your right hand out to break your fall.

Thrusting your left elbow forward, you fall down onto your stomach and then your chest. Your right arm helps ease you down and breaks the fall.

The "flat" of the left arm should be <u>next to the position you marked</u>.

Reach up with the right hand and operate the bolt and pick up the 1st round to chamber it.

You can remove the rifle from the "Mechanical Safe" position at this time.

Pick up the butt of the stock and place it into the "Pocket" of your shoulder.

Slide your right hand along the stock to the pistol grip and get a good firm grip.

Look over the rear sight and check the number board as you are coming down onto your target.

Rotate your right elbow down to the mat, into your shooting position.

Some people take the "mechanical safety" off at this point. I prefer the earlier method. I have my grip at this point and I don't want to re-adjust it.

Pick up your sight alignment as you are taking up the slack on the two stage trigger.

Take a breath and let it out to your normal respiratory pause and hold it.

Focus your vision on your front sight post.

Squeeze the trigger straight to the rear. This is the un-interrupted method. DO NOT stop. Accept your wobble area.

As the rifle fires and recoils, take your next breath. Breathe between each and every shot. DO NOT try and hold your breath for two or three shots before breathing again.

As you come back down onto your target, check to see if you are on the right target; check your number board before every shot.

Just after the first shot can be a critical point. If your pit puller is day dreaming, or yakking to a buddy, he may forget this is Rapid Fire and he will pull the target down. He wouldn't get a chance to mark it because half of the pits will jump down his throat and yell at him to get it back up in the air. In the Pits, the pullers are told to back away from the target to the wall, also not to touch the target. The Pit Officials are there to remind them

You will have to decide to either go ahead and shoot, or to call for a pit "alibi." If you go ahead and shoot, you have "accepted" the conditions and you do not rate an alibi. If you stop and raise your hand to call for the alibi, you better hope your score keeper was awake, paying attention, and doing his job so he can verify that the target did go down and come back up. A good line officer will scan the targets and watch to see if any targets were pulled on the first shot.

For the second shot, pick up your sight alignment as you take up the slack, focus, squeeze and break the shot.

The bolt will lock to the rear after the second shot. Reach up and grab the magazine and push forward on the release button with your thumb, and rotate the magazine down and forward. Lay it off to the side.

I have the second magazine with the eight rounds just off the mat on the grass. The magazine is standing straight up. The rounds are down and pointed toward the targets. It is leaning on a box of ammunition to support its upright position. The right hand grabs the bottom of the magazine that is sticking up, the thumb on the left and fingers on the right. Pick up the magazine and rotate (twist) the hand until the rounds are up and forward.

Place the magazine in the well at a slight angle, the tips of the rounds are pointed slightly up and the front end of the magazine goes in first while pushing up.

Rotate the back up until it locks. Make sure you can hear it and feel it

Reach up and place your finger on the bolt handle but do not release the catch yet.

Turn your head a little to the left and look in your spotting scope. The scope should be adjusted to the correct height and just close enough that a head movement is all that is required. See if you can pick up the first two shots, and determine if you need an elevation or wind change. *Caution:* Do Not spend too much time looking for the shot or you could save a round later. If you can see them and make a change, you may just save yourself a lot of points. Make your decision.

Release the catch and let the bolt go home before trying to make a change on the windage knob. It will get the handle out of the way. DO NOT try and scope the shots before you make the magazine change. If you run into any trouble on the magazine change, you can skip the scope. If you have already scoped and now run into trouble on the magazine change, those extra seconds can be critical.

The bolt has gone home, you have adjusted the sights, now place the rifle back in your shoulder, regain your grip, look over the sights and check your number board, rotate the elbow down into position, pick up your sight alignment, breathe, relax, focus, take up the slack, squeeze off the shot, un-interrupted, accept your wobble area, recover and do it again.

Count your shots as you shoot and remember to breathe between each shot.

As soon as the last shot is fired, and the bolt stays to the rear, look back in the spotting scope for your group. Checking the group does several things. If you see your group and you need a slight dope change, you will know how to adjust if they call a line or pit alibi, and you have to re-fire. That point is important because the pits paste the shots without showing the groups if it is a line or pit alibi. Another reason for scoping your group is, you may have a shot on or close to the line, and it helps to see it before you decide to challenge or not. When a range uses golf tees, you have to remember that the head of the tee is much larger than the shank. The head maybe on or in the line, but the shank could still be well off the line.

When the targets go down, immediately make your rifle safe: magazine out, bolt open, safety on, and, place your open bolt indicator in.

Grab your pen or pencil and your data book and stand by for your groups and scores.

Pay attention: as soon as your target comes up, mark your data book. Don't be yakking when they call, "Do you have your groups and scores?", you are just starting to look. You are holding up the match!

While you are waiting for your groups and scores to come up, reload your magazine for your second string.

In a practice session where the second string comes rather quickly behind the first and you barrel is still pretty hot, you may have to come up one half minute for the second string. Matches usually take awhile to mark and score (challenges, problems, etc.), and your barrel has time to cool off.

"For your second string, stand." Stand up and do it all over again.

At the end of your second string, after you have cleared your rifle and made it safe, make sure the line officer has made the line clear, that it is all right to get out of position and leave the line and your firing point. **GETTING OUT OF POSITION BEFORE THE LINE HAS BEEN CLEARED IS A SAFETY VIOLATION.**

As soon as the line is cleared, and before the targets come up for score, GET YOUR GEAR OFF THE LINE. The next relay needs that time to set up its gear. A competitor gets very impatient standing there with his gear in hand while you leave your gear on the point while marking your book and gathering your brass—bad manners.

Before you go in front of the line to pick up your brass, make sure the line officer has cleared it; there may be an alibi to shoot. If you are in front of the line before it has been cleared, **HEAVEN HELP YOU, ALSO A SAFETY VIOLATION.**

Count down your elevation to make sure your sights didn't run down on you. Record your elevation and windage in your data book, NOW, before you forget!

Well, that's it for the Prone Rapid Fire position. Right now, I can think of several dozen things that could have happened during the past seventy seconds of your string. These items are covered in the class on "*Line and Pit Procedures*", (a possible future book). Before you think, "I know about line and pit procedures", there are things I did not know even after fifteen years of shooting. You learn a lot when you are the one who has to run the match.

CHAPTER SEVEN

When you coach on the Marine Corps Rifle Team they issue you a big team scope. One day after a practice at two hundred yards for a rapid fire string, I was talking to my shooter, I heard someone say "Look at the score board on target sixteen." I swung the big team scope over and on the rapid fire score board was a cartoon drawing along with the shooters score; 99-4x.

Sgt. Larry Tedders besides being a National Long Range Champion Shooter, was an excellent cartoon artist. On the score board he had drawn; a beautiful blonde, wrapped in a towel saying "For a hundred, I'll take off the towel." The targets were scored and cleared. The shooters fired their second string. When the targets came up for score, all team scopes were turned to target sixteen. Sure enough, the shooter had a 100-5x. There she was in all her glory! In one hand "Miss Piggy" held a stick with the mask of the beautiful blond. In "Miss Piggy's" other hand was a waving towel; she was yelling "Yoo-Hoo" "Yoo-Hoo."

The rules say, "<u>Sitting or Kneeling</u>," for Two Hundred Yard Rapid Fire. You <u>can</u> use the kneeling position for Two hundred yard Rapid position—you can also put fire crackers in your ears. I have seen two people use the kneeling position for Two Rapid in the past fifty years; neither had anything near an acceptable group or score.

THE SITTING POSITION

There are four basic Sitting positions: crossed ankle, crossed leg, open leg and the "Figure 4". Some people use the crossed leg position and can drive nails with it. The years I used this position, I have had some incredibly mediocre scores. The open leg position is usually reserved for people whose body configurations do not permit them to use the other three positions. Michael Maxberry is, once again, the exception to the rule. That boy actually prefers the open leg position. Just to be obstinate, he does extremely well with it.

Some of the problems shooters have with the Sitting Position are: they cannot bend over far enough, they cannot hold the legs up without quivering, and they cannot get the rifle level with the targets. Most of these problems can be taken care of with a good position.

Other coaches teach the shooting <u>positions in the order they are fired</u>. In a match, the shooter will fire the Off-Hand (Standing) 1st, the Sitting Rapid Fire, both are fired at 200 yards. The shooter will move back to 300 yards and fire the Prone Rapid fire, and then will move back to 600 yards and fire the Slow Fire Prone.

During an NRA 80 shot match; 50% of the shots fired are in the Prone Position (20 rounds from 600 yards slow fire prone and 20 rounds from 300 yard rapid fire prone). 25% or 20 rounds are fired 200 yards sitting rapid fire. The remaining 25% is fired standing at 200 yards.

The reason I'm covering the positions in <u>reverse of the normal shooting order</u> is **the "Flat" of the arm is important to the Prone and Sitting Positions**. Remember my four step theory: (1) find the flat of the arm; (you have already done that) (2) get the feel of the position with-out the shooting gear; (3) dry fire the position with the equipment and mark your sling; and, (4) live fire on the range and adjust the sling while testing for group size.

I am going to use step two while describing the Sitting Position.

NRA Rule 5.10 Sitting: *Weight of the body supported on the buttocks and the feet or ankles, no other portion of the body touching the ground. The rifle will be supported by both hands and one shoulder only. Arms may rest on the legs at any point above the ankles.*

BODY PLACEMENT

The first thing you have to do is orient your body in relation to the firing line and the target. You are going to form several angles. The Apex, or point of the angles, will be you, more specifically, your butt. You have to picture this as if you were on the firing line. First, draw a line from your target to your firing point. You sit on your firing point at the end of that line you have just drawn. Now draw an imaginary line from where you are sitting on the firing line to the large number end of the firing line. This forms a ninety degree angle.

Your feet are now stretched out in front of you and pointed to the right. How much to the right? Half way on that ninety degree angle is forty-five degrees. The line formed by your feet should be slightly less than the forty-five degrees. Anywhere between thirty and forty degrees. That angle is the line from the target to the one formed by your outstretched legs. This is only a starting point. You will adjust your legs (and the angle) when you get down into position. You get the position first, and then adjust for the natural point of aim.

THE CROSSED ANKLE POSITION

Using your living room carpet and your shooting mat, you will go through the mechanics of the position. Pick out a distant spot on the wall and put a black circle on a sticky note. This is your target. Sit down. To your right, ninety degrees from the target, is the big end of the firing line. Now extend your legs flat on the floor (Fig. 32); they should be about thirty or forty degrees from the target. The exact number of degrees do not matter; it is ball park figure.

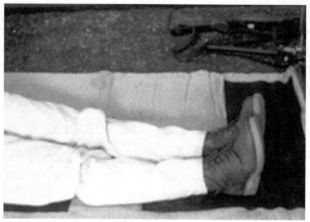

Heels Flat on the mat
Fig. 32

This position is for right handed shooters. Lift your left leg and cross it over the right leg (Fig. 33); lay it on the right leg at the ankle. The right leg is still flat on the floor. The heel of your right boot (always wear high top military-type boots for increased ankle support) is resting on the floor with your foot straight up. Now turn your right leg and foot to the right until your left heel also touches the floor.

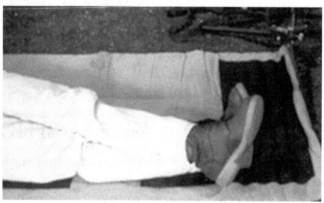

Left leg crossed over the right
Fig. 33

Pull your knees back towards your body, slowly. You will only bring them back a little. When your legs come back, your feet can rotate down until your ankles are almost flat on the floor. The toe of your right foot (now on the left side because of the crossed ankles) is resting at the instep of the left foot.

Pull your legs back only far enough to allow the feet to rotate down Fig 34. Pulling your feet back further will hurt rather than help. If you stop when the feet can lay flat, your legs will rest naturally, and you are using bone support. If you pull your legs back more, you lose bone support, and your legs will sag down. You will now use your leg muscles to raise them; and your legs start to quiver.

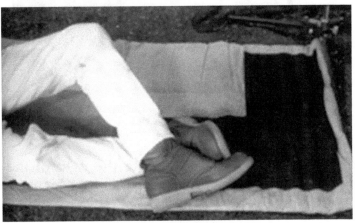

Legs drawn back
Fig. 34

Bending forward may be a problem for some people, and it can make the difference if you can use this position or not. Even if you have just a slight paunch, loosening the belt buckle may help.

Earlier we located the "flat" of the arm. Now you have to locate the "pocket" of the leg Fig. 35. If you are wearing a pair of trousers with a nice crisp crease down the front, which would go down the center line of your legs. That center line goes down past the knee and down the center of your shin bone.

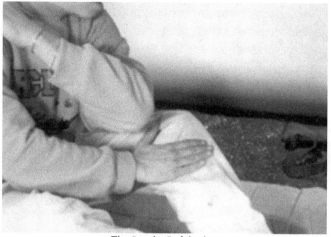

The "pocket" of the leg
Fig. 35

Just below your knee cap, and just to the right of the center line, you can feel the "pocket". It helps if your leg is stretched out, but bent slightly.

The bone just below the pocket and just to the right of the center line is relatively flat. When you bend forward, place the "flat" of the left arm on the area of the left leg just below the "pocket". The two areas fit together like a hand and a glove.

Your left forearm naturally forms an angle upward, and your hand is where the rifle rests.

There is another smaller pocket on the right leg. To the left and up the leg about an inch above the knee is the pocket your right elbow will rest in. Your cheek will rest on your right thumb for now.

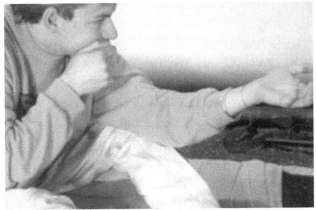

The crossed ankle position (without equipment)
Fig. 36

You now have a good solid crossed ankle position.

The crossed ankle position (with equipment)
Fig. 37

You now have good bone support without having to hold up the legs. If your imaginary rifle is pointed off to one side, you can align to your target by lifting your butt and moving it left or right, changing the angle of your legs.

I have fired a 100-9X with the crossed ankle position, and I feel comfortable with it.

SHORT STOCKING

The Match Rifle has an adjustable hand stop that can be moved to where you need it, and locked into place. Your hand is then as far forward as possible and will not slip. You hold the rifle in the position you want.

The Service Rifle does not have an adjustable hand stop. To maintain the rifle on a natural and level position, you may have to <u>short stock</u> (Move your left hand back, away from the sling swivel and hold it in place). If you put your left hand all the way forward to the sling swivel, you may find the muzzle of your rifle pointed down to the ground. To raise the barrel to level, you will have to pull your left hand back, or short stock the rifle. Keeping the hand from slipping during Rapid Fire used to be a problem. Now with a good spray of Hawkeye adhesive grip on the glove and stock, your hand will not slip.

Short Stocking, note forward hand position on stock and
how the fingers curl back towards the shooter.
Fig. 37B

THE CROSSED LEG POSITION

The crossed leg position (with equipment)
Fig.38

I'm covering this position briefly. I have shot the crossed leg position for years and never did it very well. I had a cant (Tilting the rifle to one side) that would make a seasoned sailor sea sick.

When I sat in the living room and got the position so I could describe it here, I discovered what I consider a major disadvantage to this position as compared to the crossed ankle. I'll cover it shortly.

The crossed leg position starts the same as the crossed ankle. After the left foot is crossed over the right, you pull the legs in tight and tuck them in like an Indian sitting position.

The heel of the right foot is under the left thigh, and the heel of the left foot is under the right leg just below the knee. This gives a very stable position.

Here is the disadvantage. Physically, you cannot use the "flat" of the arm to make contact just below the knee. You have to use the side of the arm next to the "flat". This gives you less surface area in contact with the leg, and a far greater chance for slippage. I think people overcome this by using the shooting pants. They have the pads to help stop the slippage. I hate them; they are a pain. Like I said, Uncle Bob, does very well with this position (he uses the shooting pants).

THE OPEN LEG POSITION

The Open leg position
Fig. 39

People of large size, people with large guts (and Lanky Mitchell Maxberry), use the open leg position. This position is almost identical to the crossed ankle except the ankles are not crossed and the legs are drawn back a little more so you do not have to bend over as far. The placement of the arms on the legs is the same as in the crossed ankle position.

In one version of the open leg position the heels are close together. The other version has the feet spread wider apart.

The "Figure Four" Position

Over the years I have found the "Figure 4" position to be about the most stable of the sitting positions. During my one week class, I teach the following sitting positions; crossed ankle, cross leg, open leg (close), open leg (wide) and Figure 4.

About four out of five students find the Figure 4 the one position that works best for them. One year during the National Matches, I noticed David Tubb using the Figure 4 position for sitting rapid.

The Figure 4 position is about identical to the crossed ankle position described earlier. Once you get into the crossed ankle position simply move your right foot back under your left leg until the instep/ankle of your right foot is supporting the left leg at the calf. This is a very stable position with good "Bone Support".

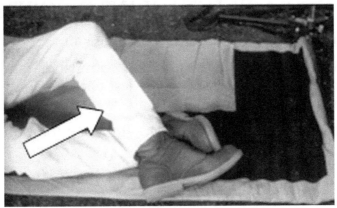

Right foot drawing back
Fig. 40

MARKING YOUR POSITION

I use a piece of brass to mark my Sitting Position. I place it at the "V" formed by the leg and the right side of my shooting jacket as it flares away from the leg. A "helpful" score-keeper removed the piece of brass because he was afraid I was going to sit on it and did not know that I used it to mark my position. (After that string of fire, we both went to the hospital. Him for the surgery and me to get my boot back!) Some people mark their position just between their legs, near their crotch. I find the other method easier to see as I go down into the sitting position.

CMP Only
"SHOOTERS STAND"

When you stand up, keep your feet as close "in place" as much as you can. I uncross my ankles and I keep my left foot in place. I draw my right leg back close to my body and by using the shooting stool close to my right side, I pushed up with my right leg and right hand on the stool into a standing position.

GOING BACK DOWN INTO POSITION

The commands are the same as the Three Rapid.

"Staying relaxed", "listening to the commands" and all the other principals discussed in the last chapter, are the same. When a target moves you can start down into position.

Pull the right foot back and behind the left foot four or five inches.

Lower your body straight down until your butt touches the heel on your right foot.

Shift your weight back and put your right hand out to break your fall. Lower yourself down to the mat. Make sure you come back to your marked position.

Make sure the muzzle is pointed down range at all times.

Place your right foot next to the left and re-cross your ankles. Continue to re-establish your position.

The sequence of events described in the last chapter, are the same for the Sitting Rapid.

Once again, this is basic information and there are many other ways of doing things. You may have to alter the position to suit your body configuration or needs. Half the fun is experimenting. The other half is finding what "Feels Good." Charlie Milazzo said "This is a book on positions, it should be rated X." I told him "Actually, it's rated 10-X."

CHAPTER EIGHT

E veryone knew the Major was a weight lifter, and he made Magilla Gorilla look like a ninety pound weakling. It came as no surprise when he walked into the classroom with an M-14 sticking straight out, horizontally, from his right shoulder, supported only by his right hand gripping the small of the stock, and his right elbow was held high away from his body. His left hand hung down by his side.

Recreation of "Major Idiot"
Fig. 41

What did come as a surprise was his pronouncement, "You must be able to hold the rifle like this, unsupported by the left arm, to shoot a good off-hand score." The members of the class looked at each other and you could hear one collective thought go up. "Keep your mouth shut. This is a public setting and military protocol prohibits us from calling you, a Bozo.

This is what we think of you and your statement. We all know you're not a rifle shooter! The Off-Hand Champion could not do this position to save his life." The basis of any position is bone support, not muscle strength.

The Off-Hand Position

The NRA rule book says, *"Both feet flat on the ground with no other part of the body touching the ground. The rifle is to be supported by one shoulder and both hands only."* I think we can go into a little more detail than that.

First, let's orientate our position to the line. Again, draw an imaginary line from the target to (and past) the firing line. Your feet will be placed **on this** line about shoulder width apart. Your body is facing toward the big end (The large numbers) of the line if you're right handed, and the little end (the smaller numbers) if you're a south paw.

Your legs should be straight but not "locked". The knees should be slightly flexed.

Anyone who has been in the military and stood inspections, knows that if you lock your knees, you will pass out. Bending the knees slightly will prevent you from landing on your face. Remember you could be in the off-hand position for twenty-five minutes or more.

The hips should be level and the body held erect. You may want to bend back slightly. We did have a Warrant Officer who bent back to an extreme amount and he shot very well with it. He was on my target one day as I was coaching. I said, "They sent me down here to straighten up your Off-Hand position." He had no sense of humor.

The head should be held erect. I found myself, and a lot of other people, stretching the neck forward to get closer to the sight, to get the "normal" eye relief. One year at Camp Perry, I was shooting rather poorly in the Off-hand position, so after six or seven shots, I moved my head back a little on the stock. This gave me less eye relief, but I started to shoot a lot better. I had less "apparent movement", and better control.

You **must point the rifle down range** when placing a round in the magazine well AND when you chamber the round

You cannot have a round in the rifle or magazine unless the rifle is pointed down range (An upward angle of 30-40 degrees is OK when placing the rifle in the shoulder).

You can no longer let the rifle rest on the stool. If you need to rest between shots and the rifle is loaded, you can cradle it in your arms with the muzzle pointed down range or you can un-load the live round and rest the rifle on the stool.

Get a firm grip on the small of the stock and pay particular attention to the placement of the hand so it is the same each and every time.

Place the butt of the stock in the "pocket" of the right shoulder. Look at the shoulder pad as you place the stock to insure that it is placed in the same spot each time.

Now place your left hand (there is a lot more to come on the placement of the left hand), where you want it, and rotate the rifle down into position. The right hand has a good firm grip, pretty much like a firm hand shake. Too tight of a grip and the hand starts to shake.

When most of the weight was supported by the right hand, the right elbow was held very high. Again, this puts a lot of muscle strain on the arms. Today the good Off-Hand shooters let the right elbow hang naturally. It will be either held horizontal or it may hang down slightly.

The Left Hand

Up until now, the Off-Hand position has been pretty much the same for most shooters. When it comes to the placement of the left hand, you will see a wide range of choices. Some are good, some are all right, and some are plain ridiculous.

The desired placement is as close to the center of balance as you can get. This gives you the bone support needed and the rifle doesn't feel "top" heavy.

The M-14/M1A has the twenty round magazine directly below the center of balance, which makes for some interesting variations on the hand placement.

Left Hand; Holding the Bottom of the Magazine

I never liked holding the rifle on the bottom of the magazine. One time some years ago a shooter on the Marine Corps Rifle Team was shooting Off-Hand and he was holding the bottom of the magazine with his left hand. When the rifle blew up, most of the force came out the bottom of the magazine. He said he always wears a shooting glove now.

Left Hand; Holding the Front of the Magazine

I find that griping in front of the magazine to be a pretty good choice. The point where the front of the magazine and the bottom of the stock meet is a ninety degree angle. The web of the left hand is placed at this juncture and can be pulled back into the shoulder in case the wind is blowing rather hard.

Web of hand meets magazine & stock
Fig. 42

Left Hand; Holding Behind the Magazine

One position I used for years was one I never saw anyone else use. It worked for me and I shot my best Off-Hand scores using it. You cannot use this position on a windy day; it must be calm. I have placed my left hand behind the magazine. It was **between the magazine and the trigger guard**. The fingers must be curled down or the bolt will tear off some skin. The left hand should be bent toward you and the web of the hand placed between the magazine and the trigger guard. This gets the hand closer to the center of gravity and gives better bone support to the position.

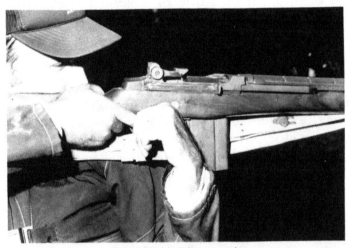

Left hand behind the magazine
Fig. 43

Left Hand; Rifle resting on Finger Tips

One of the other methods I have tried with little or no success, is to rest the rifle on the finger tips. The thumb is spread as far as possible away from the fingers, and the rifle rests on the outstretched thumb and fingers. The hand is stretched tight and there is a lot of muscle tension.

The Best Method
(With a Bolt Gun or an M-1 Garand)

I shoot a Bolt Rifle, and there is no magazine extending below the rifle. This allows me to get centered under the center of balance, and to provide bone support. But leave it to me to still find a poor position. I tell people the only reason I can teach these classes is I have done everything wrong that there is to be done. I know where all the mistakes are.

I use to curl my left wrist forward; the thumb was to the left of the stock and the fingers were to the right. I could shoot fair with this position. It was one of several I used. One year at Camp Perry, I was having one of those bad strings. After six or seven rounds, I knew it was time to change something. I switched to my other position and the shots started to go right.

This is the position I changed to: I bent my left wrist back as far as it will go. The palm of the hand is facing up. The rifle rests in the palm. The fingers and the thumb are to the left of the stock. This puts the stock in the middle of the palm, rather than on the heel. I prefer the thumb to the left. I had the best control with this position, along with moving the head back on the stock a little.

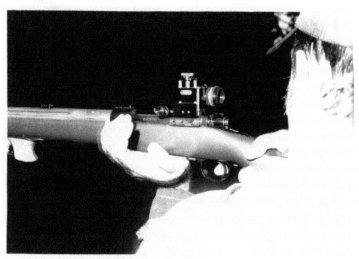

Left wrist bent back, fingers to the left
Fig. 44

"Artificial Support."

Years ago the left arm could not rest or even touch the side of your body. It was considered "Artificial Support." A line official would come up to you and place his hand between your body and the left arm. When the left arm is away from the body, it forces you to hold the rifle further forward and away from the center of balance. You lose the "Bone Support", and you are forced to use muscle tension.

This story has been around for at least fifty years or more. It has to be considered an "Urban Legend", because no one can say for sure they saw it happen. The story goes some-thing like this: A buxom female Army shooter at Camp Perry was said to have tucked her left breast under her left arm. When challenged for artificial support, she produced it and loudly proclaimed, "Does this look artificial to you?"

Now that the left arm can rest against your side (who knows, maybe she was a pioneer in the sport), you can move your left hand back on the stock. This gets you closer to the center of balance, giving you better bone support, and there is less muscle tension.

Artificial Support
Fig. 45

In an earlier chapter, I talked about a NRA classified expert who was using artificial support. What he did was take a couple of the red inserts from a box of Federal ammunition, and strung them on a web belt. He had ten rounds on each side of his body. As he was getting his Off-Hand position, the last thing he did was to <u>raise his left elbow and rest it on the ammunition pouch</u>. That is artificial support.

Be careful with the sling wrapped around your wrist, a line official can warn you for artificial support.

The "Hinged" butt plate on an M1A/M-14 may not be used in the up position, and that also is artificial support.

The <u>AR-15 Service Rifle MAY NOT rest on the top of the shoulder</u>. It is considered a safety violation. It does not have to be <u>completely in the shoulder.</u> As long as the toe (Bottom of the butt plate, part near the sling swivel) cannot be seen from behind the shooter it is considered in the shoulder.

For both NRA and CMP matches, for the Off-Hand (Standing) position only and for Service Rifles only (M-14/M1A, M-16/AR-15 and M-1 Garand) the <u>sling must be attached to both the front and rear sling swivels</u> and may or may not be included in the grasp of the left hand.

Mental Conditioning

Even if you have a good Off-Hand position, **you can defeat yourself in an instant, with your mind.**

Henry Ford said "If you think you can or if you think you can't, you are right." You must think positively and know you can do it. Most new shooters make the same mistakes, they KEEP SCORE IN THEIR HEAD.

As he takes each shot, he says to himself, "I have a one eighty - seven going", and on the next shot he says to himself, "I can still make a one eighty-five." I know this is true because I did it myself!

Warrant Officer Nogazimea told a pretty young woman Marine how to solve that problem, "Take a couple of short sharp sticks, put them down into your boots, and wrap your toes around them."

I tried a different method. I talked to myself; I told myself, "This shot will be a center shot, a ten or an X." By working on each shot, one at a time, and mentally conditioning yourself to make each shot a center one, you will solve the problem of keeping score in your head, and will maintain the proper mental conditioning at the same time. The scores will take care of themselves; they will be there when you are finished, and they may just be a pleasant surprise.

If you are thinking an X or a ten on each shot, and the old doubts come back and you think a nine or even out of the black, **TAKE THE RIFLE DOWN AND START OVER**. Take the round out and start with a new one. That negative thought is an alarm bell; ignore it and you will wish you hadn't.

Every time you shoot Off-Hand, think of the highest score you have ever shot in a match or in practice; tell yourself, "I'm going to beat that score." You are shooting against yourself; your own previous scores. You are not shooting against the other people on the firing line.

DON'T QUIT! When the weather turns bad and the people who shoot better than you start to give up, you will be the winner simply by hanging in there.

The Grand Finale

I am going out on a limb—again. I am going to give you a five step process that will **raise your Off-Hand scores from three to ten points,** or more, depending on your present average. If your average is 192 or lower, this theory should produce the results I have stated here. It's not that difficult to raise your average.

The pioneers, with their covered wagons and horses, found the traveling on a prairie not too difficult. When crossing the Rockies, they first came to the foot hills. The start of the climb wasn't too bad. The higher they got into the mountains, the steeper the climb and the slower the progress.

If you are shooting below the 180's, you are still on the prairie. If you are in the 180's, you are still in the foot hills. When you get into the 190's, your rate of increase will start to slow. Once you are in the upper 190's, you are getting near the top of the mountain, and you are going to have to scratch for every inch.

All of the steps have been covered before, either in the Sight Alignment Book, or in this book. We are going to go over each step again, and put it all together.

Step One

Re-read the section on the **trigger control exercise** in the Sight Alignment Book. Don't just do it a few times, do it HUNDREDS of times, and do it until you can take up one half the trigger pull and hold it each and every time. **Do the exercises every night for One Hour for three Months.** Your Off-Hand average WILL go up. One of my students did this exercise one hour every night for three months and his scores went from the 450s to the 480s.

Step Two

Re-read the section on **"Natural Point of Aim"** in the Sight Alignment Book.. When you are on the firing line, make sure you apply it and remember KEEP YOUR FEET IN PLACE.

Step Three

Re-read the section on **Focus** in the Sight Alignment Book. Use the yellow paint on the front sight as described in the Sight Alignment Book and draw the scratch in the paint. By focusing on the scratch EVERY SHOT, your averages will go up in all your positions.

Step Four

Re-read the section on the **Sub-Six Hold** in the Sight Alignment Book. Here is the BIG change and the most controversial — some of the older shooters do not like my saying this. "Stop trying to use a 6 o'clock hold."

People say "the 6 o'clock hold gives you a defined aiming point." That is true, but most people try to use that defined aiming point in the Off-Hand position, and they try too hard to make the shot perfect. Along with their poor trigger control, they start jerking the trigger.

This is for Off-hand only. "Use a sub-six hold." On a four foot by six foot target, the aiming black is in the center. I want you to aim "about" half way from the 6 o'clock position of the aiming black to the bottom of the target. There is a lot of white area there. Maintain your sight alignment, your focus, your natural point of aim, and your trigger control.

Most people have to "push up" with the left hand to get the barrel (and the sights) to the 6 o'clock position. The front end of the rifle wants to hang down, and your arm feels more natural. By using the sub-six hold, you can let it hang down and make use of this natural feel.

Step Five

"Accept your Wobble Area." The rifle will wobble around a little—let it—accept it (I said "Accept" it, don't be proud of it). If you follow the other steps and accept your wobble area, you will be amazed at how much better you will shoot.

With the sub-six hold, you are aiming at a larger area, not a very fine point. The Marine Corps Pistol Team uses a technique that helps new shooters. They will take a pistol target and glue it to the cardboard backward. There is no bulls eye to aim at. All the shooter has is the center of the white paper. He now works on his sight alignment, focus, trigger control, and his wobble area.

We shoot a local fun match and I like to try different techniques. I had my 24 power scope on my AR-15. We shot the National Match Course, reduced for 200 yards. Who needs drugs? Shooting Off-hand with a 24 power scope is a trip. I have a wobble area the size of Cleveland. Every shot "Looked" horrible (8's and 7's), but because I accepted my wobble area, the shots were coming up X's, tens and nines.

One Last Story
The "Gang" goes out for Chinese food on Saturday nights; we catch up on what is going on and swap lies. Jon Wilcox is a lawyer who can make a functional illiterate look like an author. Jon said, "I thought of you on my last prairie dog hunt." The story went something like this. Jon and his partner had been shooting prairie dogs from the prone position, and at great distances. There was a "village" about fifty yards from their position, but due to the terrain, Jon could not see the prairie "village" from the prone position.

When he stood up for an Off-Hand shot, a dog was bouncing all over the cross hairs of his scope. Jon said "I could hear you in the class—Accept your wobble area."

"IT WORKS!" He said.

CHAPTER NINE

Service Rifle Leather Sling

1st Sgt. Steve Allermann, United States Marine Corps Reserve, decided he wanted to take up competitive shooting. He borrowed an M1A from Bill Wallis to shoot the State Championships. Steve believes the tighter the sling, the better; "You can't have a sling too tight," says he. Now most people, when in the prone position, will take the rifle out of their shoulder, the butt of the stock will rest on the shooting mat and the muzzle will naturally form an upward angle. Not Steve! His sling is sooo tight that the muzzle points down to the ground and the butt of the stock point's upward. It's about 18 inches above his right shoulder. He has to reach up and force the rifle down and into his shoulder. When he did this on the borrowed rifle, the upper sling swivel popped out of the wood. Steve came back to Bill with the sling and swivel in one hand and the rifle in the other. He asked, "Do you have another rifle? This one broke!" Steve later claimed the stock was defective. I didn't think that was the case, but it does bring up a point about equipment (sling). My rule of thumb is, "BUY THE BEST EQUIPMENT YOU CAN AFFORD." You can upgrade later if need be. What amazes me is the people who have a $900 to $1500 rifle, and use a $20 sling.

The point is, there are some slings on the market that I would not carry my rifle with for fear the hooks would straighten out and the rifle would fall and damage the sights. I saw one of these slings at Camp Perry in 1993. Made and sold by two reputable companies, both of which carry some excellent products. I don't believe either would cheat the shooting community (their bread and butter); I am hoping it is an honest mistake. People tend to get very testy when you tell them that their product isn't worth a hill of beans. This particular sling has the type of hooks that will straighten out if a little too much pressure is applied. Moreover, the leather is too thin. It's more for show than for use - yet it was selling for nearly $30.

Leather slings, like cars, come in different sizes, shapes and price ranges. The two best Service Rifle leather slings that I recommend are the ones made by **Richard Turner** of Turner Saddlery, P.O. Box 120, Clay, Alabama, 35048. (205) 680-9377, www.turnersling.com ...and by **Leslie Tam**, 1411 Saint Louis Dr., Honolulu, HI 96816, (808) 737-5427, www.lestam.com .

You won't need a new one every year or so. Both have excellent quality and professional workmanship, and will last. They are both hand stitched, with wide keepers; like the Tam sling, the holes are numbered. Richard Turner coats his slings with a product called "Turner Saddlery Military Leather Dressing," it's a mixture of bear grease and bees wax. This gives an excellent protection to the leather. His slings are 50 inches long rather than the standard 48 inches. The longer length comes in handy for the people with long arms and for those who shoot the AR. He will make the sling longer upon request at a dollar per inch up to maximum of four inches

Brownells, Inc., 200 S. Front Street, Montezuma, IA 50171, has a very good sling.(Brownell's Competitor Plus) I have not used one, but from what I have seen, they meet all requirements and I recommend them.

I don't know who makes the MRT Sling (Mildew Resistant Treatment). On someone's recommendation, I used one and I consider it the minimum acceptable sling for high power: It stretches quite a bit. You would need a new one every year. The hooks are good, and the keepers are OK.

Hunting type slings are for carrying a hunting rifle only, not for competitive shooting. I consider the web sling to be inadequate for high power competition. But again, for a dissenting opinion, please see Chapter Two.

Reference Points

My mother-in-law had a rather unique way of giving instructions. Twenty feet before the intersection, at fifty-five mph, she yells, "Turn here!" It came as no surprise when I read a letter my wife had written giving instructions to some friends on how to get to our place. "Turn right at the sign." I pointed out the sign was only six inches square and was one hundred yards after the turn.

When giving instructions, one must have reference points - things people can easily see, well in advance of the turn, i.e., the numbers, street signs, shopping centers, stores, gas stations, bars, etc. When these reference points are linked, they provide an easy and clear road map to your destination.

The leather sling has many reference points. We orientate these one to another, thus placing the sling on the rifle and using it effectively becomes less of a mystery.

To begin, take the leather sling off the rifle and disassemble it into the four pieces.

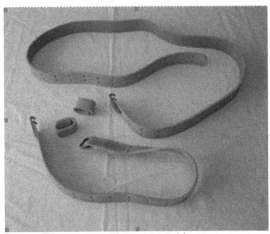

(Long strap, Short strap & 2 keepers
Fig. 46

You should have a long strap, short strap and two "Keepers."

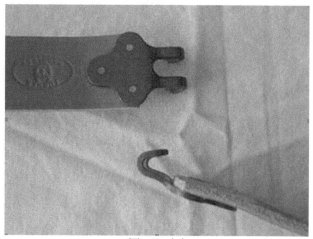

(The Hooks)
Fig. 47

Each of the straps will have a set of hooks, or "frogs," on one end. Both straps have a smooth and a rough side.

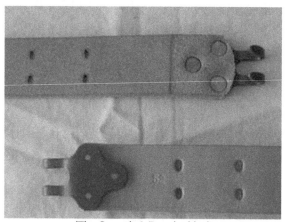

(The Smooth & Rough sides)
Fig. 48

The hooks always curl toward the rough side. If you put the strap down on the floor with the hooks pointed down, the rough side will face down, the smooth side facing up.

Both straps have a series of holes. You will find on a new sling, the holes are so extremely tight that it's difficult to get the hooks into the holes. As you use the sling, you will find the set of holes you use the most, become so enlarged that the hooks fall out and will not hold (time to replace the sling or use another set of holes).

The long strap has the hooks on one end. There's a series of holes in the first one-third the length of the sling; in the second third, there are no holes. For the remaining third, there is yet another series of holes. On the far end, the strap is cut off and rounded. With a pencil, mark this end "A." (Fig. 4) It will keep me from having to say, "the cut off and rounded end" every other line.

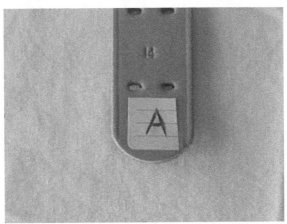

(The cut off and rounded end marked as "A")
Fig. 49

The short strap has the hooks at one end and a "D" ring at the other. The set of holes run the entire length of the short strap.

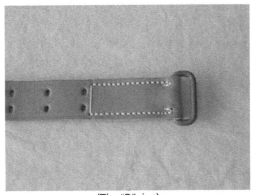

(The "D" ring)
Fig. 50

The remaining two items are the "keepers." They look like large belt loops.

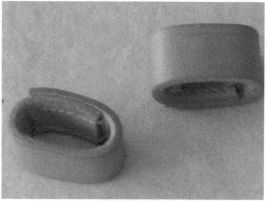

(The 2 keepers)
Fig. 51

Each year I fired the Marine Corps Division Matches, we would draw all of our shooting equipment, including the leather sling, use it for the six weeks and turn it in upon check out. As we looked through the box of hundreds of leather slings, each one having been used by dozens of previous shooters, hundreds of times, we attempted to pick out the best of the worst.

The "keepers" would be stretched beyond belief. One little trick we learned was to cut the stitching with an Exacto blade, and wrap the keepers tightly around the sling and re-sew them with dental floss. Another problem was that the slings were so stretched that the sets of holes would be so far apart that one set made a sling too tight, and the next set made it too loose. We would take an empty .22 caliber shell and a hammer, and make a new set of holes between the old holes.

Assembling the Sling

You do not need much space to lay the sling out each time you work with it, but for the first time, Here is the step-by-step procedure; the extra room is only required for clarity of description.

Kneel down in the middle of your living room rug. Draw an imaginary line from the wall on your left to the wall on your right; have it pass in front of your knees. If your imagination isn't that good, have someone lay a string out in front of you from left to right.

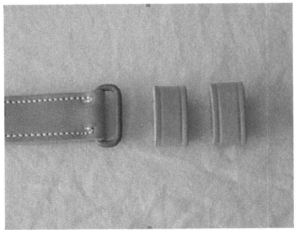

(Short strap, hooks down)
Fig. 52

On this imaginary line, lay the short strap, hooks down and to your left. The "D" ring should be directly in front of you. Place the two "keepers," <u>stitching down</u>, on the line just to the right of the "D" ring. If one keeper is a little larger or looser, see if it accommodates three thicknesses of leather; the other one accommodates only two thicknesses. Place the larger one to the right of the other keeper (Fig.52). Now, place the <u>long strap, hooks up</u>, on the line off to your right. The cut off and rounded end of the strap is just to the right of the keepers (Fig.53).

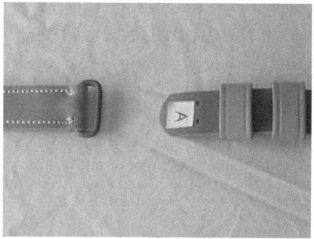

(Long strap, hooks up)
Fig. 53

Take one of the keepers and feed it onto the long strap at "A"; Pull it down to the 2nd series of holes (closest to the hooks), about the middle. (Fig. 54).

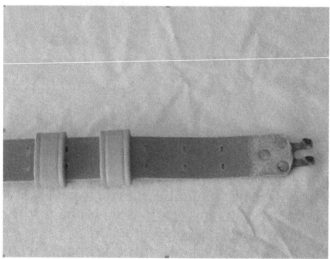

(Keepers moved up the long strap, near the hooks)
Fig. 54

Take the second keeper and feed it onto the long strap at "A," and pull it up to the first keeper. Take the "D" ring and turn it up toward the ceiling with your left hand. Feed the long strap at "A" through the "D" ring to the left (Fig. 55).

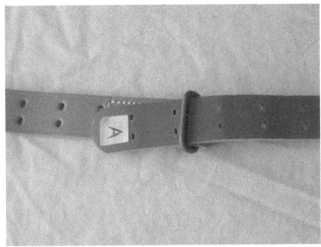

(Long strap through the "D" ring
Fig. 55

Keep moving the "D" ring to the right along the long strap until it is 6 to 8 inches from the keepers. Take the long strap at "A" in your left hand and bend it back toward the right, over the "D" ring. The smooth side will now be up (Fig 56).

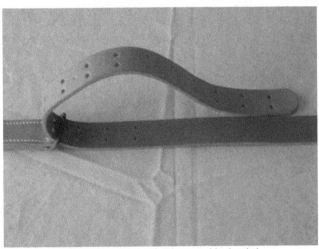

(Curl the long strap back toward its hooks)
Fig. 56

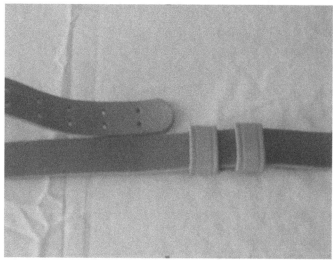

(Bring the 2 keepers about 1/2 way back)
Fig. 57

With the two keepers close together, place the thumb of your right hand along the side of the two keepers. Place the second and third finger on the side away from you. This will hold the keepers steady. Take the long strap, two or three holes below "A," in your left hand and feed "A" through both keepers, holding them firm with your right hand. Keep feeding until "A" is an inch or so through the keepers (Fig. 58).

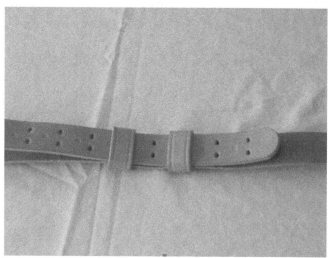

(Feed the long strap through the keepers)
Fig. 58

Now pull the bottom portion of the strap to the left and the top portion of the strap to the right (Fig. 59). Now switch hands and hold the keepers tightly, in the same manner as you did with the right hand. Pull the long strap at "A" with your right hand far past the hooks.

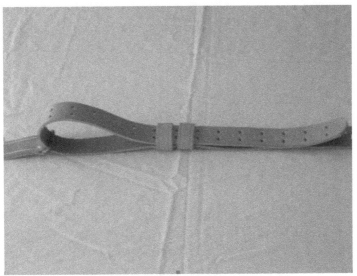

(Pull the bottom to the left & the top to the right)
Fig. 59

At this point turn the sling over, the hooks on the long strap are now facing down (Fig. 60)

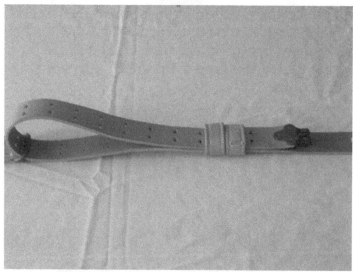

(The loop shown is the part that will go on your arm)
Fig. 60

Now take the long strap and curl it back toward the keepers, then slide it under the hooks (Fig. 61). Now place the hooks into a set of holes (3rd or 4th set from the end, <u>for now</u>, when you dry-fire later, you will determine the right set of holes)

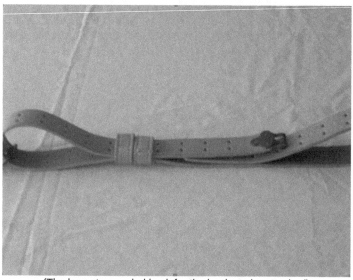

(The long strap curled back for the hooks to be attached)
Fig. 61

Next take the hooks on the short strap and curl it up and place them into the set of holes just below the other set of hooks (Fig. 62)

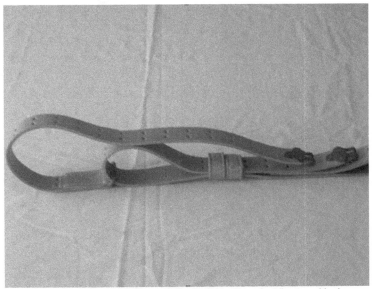

(The short strap curled up placing it in the "Parade Sling" position)
Fig. 62

At this point the "D" ring should be about 6 to 8 inches below or to the left of the keepers. Congratulations!! The sling is now assembled and ready to be placed on the rifle.

Someone is going to say, "That's not the way I do it. To that person, I say "You are right; it isn't the way you do it. It is the way I teach it and the way the Marine Corps Team teaches it. It is the way the 1992 and 1993 Service Rifle Champions did it." If you are pig-headed and stubborn, go ahead and put it back the way you did in the past, it's your sling. If, however, you are open to new ways of doing things, give it a try.

The two major changes with this method are: (1) the hooks, or frogs, are on the inside, facing towards the stock rather than the out-side, facing away from the rifle, while the sling is in the "parade" position; (2) Both keepers are below the hooks. The old method had one keeper below and one keeper above the hooks.

A "Parade" Sling

When I was on active duty and standing inspections with the rifle. The leather sling had to be on the rifle and in the "Parade" position. The sling had to be attached to the upper and lower sling swivels and had to be <u>pulled tight</u> against the rifle, the hooks had to be facing <u>out</u>, away from the rifle (It looks better).

The method I have described has the hooks facing <u>in</u> towards the rifle. This is a better way of using the sling for shooting and is sometimes called "Backwards" by some people.

Fig. 63

A "Parade" sling is attached to both upper and lower sling swivels. As in Fig. 63 above the sling is then adjusted so it is TIGHT and lays flat against the stock of the rifle.

For both NRA and CMP Competition shooting, the "Offhand" or also called the "Standing" position, the rules require the sling be attached to both the upper and lower sling swivels, and basically be in a "Parade" sling position.

With the service rifle (M-1, M-14, M-16), the sling must be attached to the rifle at both sling swivels and may or may not be included in the grasp of your left hand. The sling may be moved to the right, the left or across the bottom of the magazine. Here is where the problem comes in. If you move the sling to the right of the magazine, and do not include the sling in your grasp, it will naturally wrap around the outside of your left hand if you are holding the stock forward of the magazine. An over-zealous line official can come along and warn you and/or disqualify you for having the sling wrapped around the hand, called "Artificial Support."

You can avoid this by having the sling to the left of the magazine. You can use the sling under the magazine . . . if you don't mind looking like a dork.

CHAPTER TEN

Many interesting things happen at rifle matches that have nothing to do with shooting. My Daughter and Son-in-Law came up to Camp Perry to work as N.R.A. Volunteers at the National Matches at Camp Perry, Ohio. Tom was in the Army and he was driving his brand new van, with its TV, VCR, stereo, and all the other bells and whistles. He slowly cruised the parking lot behind the 1000 yard line looking for a parking space. "You can always park next to the Marine Corps van," I said.

"Do you trust them?" He asked.

"With his life," replied my wife. I added, "But don't get too close, they will steal anything."

He hit the brakes, his head snapped around and his mouth dropped open. I smiled and said, "Both statements are true."

He then parked a discreet distance from the Marine Corps van.

The Legend continues.

Putting the Sling on the Rifle

Start by placing the rifle butt on the floor with the muzzle pointing up towards the ceiling. The sling swivels should be facing to your right. Gravity causes the upper sling swivel to hang down. Support the rifle at the upper swivel with your left hand.

Hold the stock with your thumb on one side of the stock and the fingers on the other.

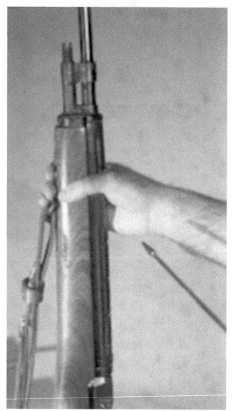

(Do not pick up the M1A or M-1 Garand by the hand guard)
Fig. 64

CAUTION: With the M1A & M-1 Garand, do not _lift_ the rifle from this position (Fig. 64). Placing the hand guard into the web of the hand and lifting the rifle could cause the hand guard to loosen, thus destroying the accuracy of your shots. Be sure to lift the rifle from the <u>underside</u>, just below the sling swivel

(Feed the strap down through the sling swivel)
Fig. 65

With the middle finger, hold the sling swivel out in a horizontal position. Now, with your right hand, hold the sling up, just above the sling swivel. With the hand about two inches below "A," (Remember, "A" is the cut off and rounded end of the long strap) bend over the end of the strap toward the rifle. Now, hold "A" a few inches above the swivel and feed it *"Down",* into the swivel (Fig. 65).

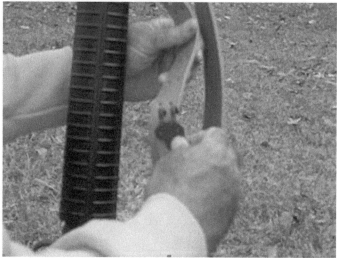

(Attach the hooks to the sling)
Fig. 66

Reach forward and pull "A" down toward the trigger guard until it touches the trigger guard. Take the hooks on the long strap and place them into a set of holes about two or three inches below the swivel (Fig. 66).

(The long strap attached, notice <u>the leather from the hooks to the end at "A", this is "The Tail"</u>)
Fig. 67

At this point, <u>any set of holes will do</u>. We are setting up the sling for a "Parade" sling position.

Before we go on, let us review. Using the left hand hold the rifle at arm's length with butt of the rifle on the ground and letting the sling hang down. Notice the long strap forms a large "loop" (Fig. 67).

The smooth side of the sling is facing the outside of the loop, and the rough side is on the inside of the loop. The two keepers hold the loop together.

(Follow the long strap from the hooks to the end)
Fig. 68

The hooks are now close to the stock. (Fig. 68) Starting at the hooks, the <u>long strap</u> runs down, through both keepers, and down through the "D" ring. It then turns up, through both keepers again, and up to the upper sling swivel and curls back down through that swivel. It then meets the hooks and continues down to a "tail" between the loop and finally ends at "A."

(Feed the hooks of the short strap up)
Fig. 69

Now take the hooks on the <u>short strap</u> and hold them close to the floor. <u>Feed the hooks up through the lower sling swivel</u> (Fig. 69) and pull the strap up.

(Pull the short strap up)
Fig. 70

(Place the hooks just below the other set)
Fig. 71

Hook it into the set of holes just below the first set of hooks (Fig. 71). The sling is now attached to the rifle, intentionally loose.

Tighten the Sling to a "Parade" Position

(Sit back on the right heel)
Fig. 72

How to tighten the sling to a "Parade" position. Both hands must be free. The best way is to kneel down with the left foot flat on the floor, and sit back onto the heel of the right foot (Fig. 72). Place your left hand under the upper swivel between the stock and the sling. Place your right hand at the small of the stock and rotate the strap 90 degrees so the sling is facing away from you. Move the rifle stock four to six inches away from your body and tilt the muzzle back until the rifle rests across your left shoulder. The floor is supporting the butt of the rifle. Your shoulder is supporting the upper part of the rifle, leaving both hands free to work the sling.

(Pull down on the outside & up on the inside)
Fig. 73

Place the thumb of the left hand between the stock and the sling at the point between the two sets of hooks. The fingers are placed inside the loop. Now pinch the leather with the thumb and forefinger of the left hand. The outside of the loop will not be in this pinched section. Now place your right thumb into the small section of the loop below the two keepers and above the "D" ring. The fingers of the right hand will lie outside of the loop, on the smooth side of the leather. In other words **"Pull down on the outside loop & up on the inside loop"**.

Pinch the leather with the thumb and forefinger of the your right hand. *By pulling down with the right hand and up with the left hand, you will tighten the sling to a "Parade" position (Fig. 73).*

To loosen the sling, simply pull down with the left hand and up with the right. Try it a few times and it will become second nature to you.

Another Story

The first time I met Paul was just after a practice session. Everyone went to Marty's for pizza and beer. Paul was sitting across from me; wearing a Marine Corps sweat shirt. I assumed he was a former Marine.

I was telling a story and the term "Butt Stroke" was used. Paul assumed it had something to do with homosexuals. I ask him, "Weren't you a Marine?" He said, "NO, I just bought the sweatshirt at K-Mart!" I then explained to him that "Butt stroke" was used in a combat situation. To "Butt stroke" is to afford the enemy the opportunity to inflict as much damage as possible to the stock, or "Butt"of your rifle, with either the side of his head or, preferably, his chin.

Uncle Bill is the only person known to have "Butt stroked" himself. Just in front of the 600 yd. line is a slight down hill curve. Uncle Bill had just put the sling on his arm and he was kneeling near the top of the curve, facing away from the targets. His leg started to cramp from kneeling so long; he took a step back, and lost his balance. He threw his left arm out to break the fall.

The sling, being attached to his arm on one end, and the rifle on the other, caused him to "Butt stroke" himself right along side of his head.

He fell backward, ass-end over tea kettle, and came up with his glasses tilted and shaking his head. This happened some years ago. He hoped to have lived it down by now. NOT LIKELY! What are friends for?

PLACING THE SLING ON YOUR ARM

The next step is to place the sling on your arm and adjust it.

The first stage of fire in a rifle match is Off-Hand Position or Standing Position. <u>You must have the sling on the rifle attached to both sling swivels for the Off Hand Position - Service Rifles only</u>. Match Rifles may <u>remove the sling</u> for Off-hand. In Marine Corps competition, the sling must be a parade sling, i.e., TIGHT. NRA rules allow it to be loose, even under the magazine.

(Disconnect the LOWER, Short strap)
Fig. 74

You are starting with a parade sling, first step disconnect the lower of the two hooks, the ones on the short strap (Fig. 74).

The Sling may be too tight to disconnect the hooks; to correct this all you need to do is simply pull down on the inside of the long strap (the one with the hooks) and up on the outside of the loop. This will give you enough slack to disconnect the lower set of hooks.

(Connect the short strap onto itself)
Fig. 75

Pull the short strap up out and away from the rifle until the hooks are near the lower sling swivel. Re-connect the hooks to the second or third set of holes from the end of the hooks (Fig. 75).

By attaching the short strap to the lower sling swivel, you have "Gotten it out of the way." I saw a shooter let it hang loose, not connected. As he was going down into the sitting position for his string of rapid fire, the hooks got caught on one of the straps on his shooting jacket. He was about two inches short of being able to place the rifle into his shoulder.

Another method is to disconnect the short strap from the rifle completely and wrap it around the left arm at the bicep after the sling is placed on the arm. It works, but is not worth the effort. Connecting it to the lower swivel is faster and does just as well.

The best way to put the sling on your arm is while you are sitting in a chair on the shooting stool. Kneeling is also an acceptable position. While sitting place the butt of the rifle at the very top of your right leg, where the leg meets the torso of your body. Now cradle the rifle in the crook of your right arm. This leaves both hands free to work the sling. The underside of the rifle, by the trigger guard, should be facing to your left. You now have free access to the sling.

While you are putting the sling on your arm, keep one important thing in mind. When you first put the sling on the rifle, you randomly selected a set of holes for the frogs on the long strap. You now have <u>a ninety-nine per-cent chance of **not** having the correct setting</u> for your shooting position. The only way to get the correct setting is by trial and error. Putting the sling on your arm, try to get into a dry-fire position, taking the sling off your arm, re-adjusting the set of holes, and repeating the procedure again. It may take two or three attempts, but look on the bright side, it will give you practice on using the sling.

The good news is, in the section of this book on Positions, I will give you my "Four Step" Theory that will help you get the right set of holes faster.

Nine times out of ten, new shooters will start with the frogs too far up from the end of the strap, and when they put the sling on the arm and try to get down into position, it is far too tight. I suggest you count up from the end of the strap (the one we called "A") to the fifth, sixth or seventh set of holes, and try that as your starting point.

A good "rule of thumb" is to have the length of sling from the swivel to your arm equal to about the distance of your elbow to your finger tips. Again, that is a "starting" point.

(Lower half of the loop)
Fig. 76

In Fig. 76, Let's look at the "Loop" formed by the long strap. The loop is held together by the two keepers. You have to do a little mental gymnastics at this point. The strap, that part of the loop closest to the rifle (the one that has the frog, or hooks) is now considered the "Stationary" strap and the one away from the rifle is the "Moveable" strap. Yes, I know, it is one long piece of leather, but it helps to explain which side we are talking about by referring to one side as stationary and the other side as movable.

Once you hold the hooks and two keepers tight in your hand, that side of the long strap (closest to the rifle) now becomes "Stationary." The side of the long strap (away from the rifle) is free to move up and down through both the keepers and the upper sling swivel, so it becomes the "Moveable" side.

The dividing point for the two is the upper sling swivel at the top, and the "D" ring of the short strap at the bottom. The "moveable" strap or portion of the loop is outside or away from the rifle. The rough side is facing inside the loop. There is nothing but leather from the upper swivel to the "D" ring, except where it passes through the two keepers. From the keepers, down to the "D" ring is the part your arm will pass through. (Fig. 76)

The <u>stationary</u>, or fixed part of the strap or loop, is to the inside, closest to the rifle. It goes from the upper swivel down to the frog or hooks, and continues down through the keep-ers (both are below the frog) and continues down to the "D" ring of the short strap.

The only remaining part of the loop is the "Tail." It is that part of the leather that is from the frog to "A", or the cut off end of the strap.

Before you put the sling on your arm, you have to prepare it. With the rifle in the crook of your arm, and both hands free to work the sling. Take the "tail" and bend it so it faces up. The "tail" is normally facing down and it may or may not be held by the keepers. Simply slide the keepers down until the "tail" is free and bend it 180 degrees so "A" faces up towards the upper swivel. The "tail" will still be between the inner and outer straps of the loop (Fig. 33).

(The "Unit" is the 2 keepers & the hooks)
Fig.77

Slide the two keepers all the way up to the frog and the upper one should even slide onto the rounded lower portion of the metal, where the rivets hold the metal to the leather. <u>The frog and the two keepers always stay together</u> to form a <u>**"Unit."**</u> (Fig. 77) This "Unit" is the stationary portion and gives the sling its holding ability.

The Half Twist

(The sling curves around the hand)
Fig. 78

"You have to give the sling a half twist outboard in order to have the sling form naturally around your hand." (Fig.78). I have heard that statement hundreds of times over the years, and yet, I have seen a lot of people give it a half twist inboard. The problem is most people don't know what the hell you are talking about.

In the prone position, your left hand, protected with a shooting glove, should be all the way forward to the sling swivel.

You should notice the sling will curve, naturally, around the back of your left hand (Fig. 78).

If it does not curve, naturally, around the back of your left hand, you have the half twist "Backwards." The sling will be twisted the wrong direction and will not lie flat on the back of your left hand.

MAKING THE ARM LOOP

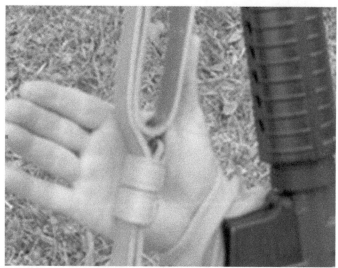

(The sling hanging straight down)
Fig. 79

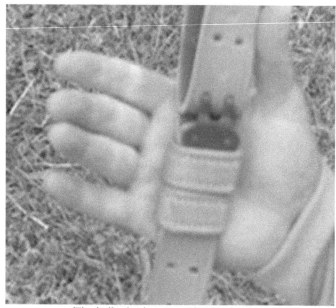

(The half twist, keepers & hooks showing)
Fig. 80

When the sling hangs from the upper swivel, the width of the sling is parallel to the width of the rifle. With your left hand, **twist the sling so that the "Unit" (the hooks and two keepers) are laying flat in your hand (Fig. 80)**. If you twisted it the wrong way, you would see the two keepers, but not the hooks.

(Gripping the unit to keep it stationary)
Fig. 81

The thumb is above the hooks and the "unit" lies in the palm of the right hand. Now wrap the fingers of the right hand around the "Unit" and get a good firm grip (Fig. 81).

The "Unit" is now held stationary with the right hand and the moveable outside strap is slid through the "Unit." By pulling down on the movable strap, held below the unit with the left hand, you can form a loop for your left arm (Fig 82).

The width of the sling is now facing towards you. To get the loop, simply bend your right wrist away from your body and use your left hand to open the loop.

(This is the loop that goes onto your arm)
Fig. 82

Placing the Sling on the Arm

(Grab the bottom of the jacket sleeve to keep it from riding up)
Fig. 83

Grip the sleeve of both the shooting jacket and the sweat shirt with the fingers of your left hand (Fig 83). This will keep the sleeves from riding up your arm as you put the sling on your arm.

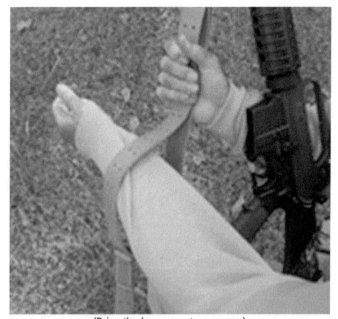

(Bring the loop up onto your arm)
Fig. 84

Place your left hand through the arm loop Fig. 84.

(Up onto the bicep)
Fig.85

Bring the loop up until it is above your left elbow and directly on your left bicep (Fig 85).

(Pull up on the outer strap while holding on to the unit)
Fig. 86

Before you get the sling on and completely adjusted, test to make sure you have the half twist outboard. It is a lot easier to change things at this point rather than later. If it is twisted, start over.

Tightening it down

(Bring the unit down close to the arm)
Fig. 87

Now that you have tested it, remove your left hand and tighten the loop on your left arm (Fig. 87).

(Push the unit away from your body by an inch or two)
Fig. 88

With your right hand holding the "unit" in a firm grip, slide the moveable strap by pulling up with your left hand. The arm loop will get smaller around your bicep. Stop pulling when the arm loop gets to be the same size as the jacket around your arm.

When the "unit" is tightened down, it will come to the top of your arm. Twist the loop on your arm until the "unit" is about an inch or two away from your body (Fig. 88).

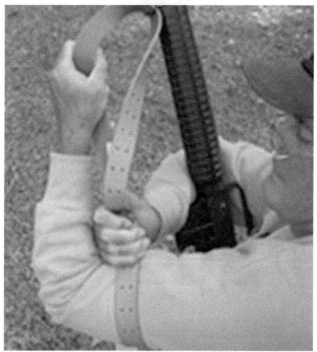

(As you tighten the sling it will come back to center)
Fig. 89

NOW, tighten the sling. With your right hand still holding the "unit" (the frog and two keepers) using a firm grip, and your left hand, pull up on the movable strap. The unit will rotate back to the center line as the sling tightens onto your upper arm about 2-4 inches above the elbow (Fig. 89).

How Tight?

My thoughts on the subject include snugging it down firmly, but not so tight that it cuts off the circulation in your arm, you don't want to feel a "Pulse beat" in your hand.

Someone told me a well-known High Power shooter advocates having the sling so tight that it is almost to the point of cutting off the circulation. It may work for him, but many other well-known shooters say it should be snug, but not so tight as to give a pulse beat. One National Champion even says you should be able to slide two fingers between the sling and your arm.

With both the Service Rifle and the Match Rifle slings, I have noticed the "unit" or buckle, will pull away from the arm an inch or so and leave a small gap. I have often wondered, "Does this affect the shooting?" We had our first Four-Gun Six Hundred Yard Championship at the La Crosse Rifle Club, and I had just finished shooting and I took a walk down the line. Both Boots Obermeyer and his son, Eric, had the small gap where the sling pulled away. Eric won the match with a score 798 out of a possible 800 points.

Leather and Cordura shooting jackets come with a shoulder strap. I believe small bore shooters use them to keep the sling from sliding down the arm. Service Rifle slings are difficult to get in and out of. Most people I know take the shoulder strap off and throw it away. I was under the mistaken impression the shoulder strap was not legal for High Power matches. They are not legal for DCM "Leg" matches.

They are legal for regular NRA matches. I only know of one person who uses it for High Power; he is lovable, but off in his own little world, and for the most part, not dangerous to himself or anyone else.

Now that you have tightened the sling on your arm, put the shooting glove on your hand. Place your hand under the stock and close to the swivel. The sling should wrap naturally around your hand.

Try getting into a prone position. Chances are you will not have the hooks in the correct set of holes. You will have to get out of position, loosen the sling from your arm, and re-adjust the hooks: up toward the swivel will tighten the sling and down on the "tail" will loosen it. After you have adjusted the sling, you will have to re-tighten the sling on your arm and try the position again.

Taking the Sling Off

To re-adjust or take the sling off of your arm, you will have to loosen the arm loop. The best way to loosen the sling is to reach around the rifle with your right hand and grab the leather just above the hooks. Pull up on it while pulling down and away from your body with your left bicep.

A DISSENTING OPINION

I have this TOTAL disdain for the web and/or the cotton sling. I was shocked to find... not everyone agrees with me.

Jack Kreiger introduced me to Mitch Maxberry at Camp Perry in 1990. The name didn't mean anything to me at the time, I found him to be a nice and likable guy. Mitchell Maxberry won the Leach Cup 1,000 yd. Iron Sight Match that year, using one of Jack's barrels.

1993 was a very good year for Mitch. He won the Air Force Cup, setting a new record. He also won the Tompkins Cup, Long Range Aggregate and the Marine Corps Cup. He has won the Kentucky State Championship five times.

Had anyone else told me the merits of the web sling, I would have ignored them. But, to ignore someone with a record as impressive as Mitchell Maxberry, would be stupid. I may be dumb, but I haven't reached down to stupid, yet.

I talked with Mitch on the phone and he gave me a pretty good list of benefits. He followed up with a letter:

Dear Jim:

I would like to give some reasons why I prefer the web sling over the leather. First let's make sure we are talking about the correct sling. The sling in reference to, is the U.S. Military sling used from WW II to early Vietnam-era. Don't confuse this sling with inferior foreign web slings which bear close resemblance and the nylon slings that slip.

One of the many advantages to the web sling is the speed and ease of adjustment and set-up, which gives the shooter more time to use during the prep time. To achieve this advantage, the sling is left on the coat at all times. In the case of the Service Rifle (for Off-Hand), a spare sling is carried with two of the hooks, one on each end of the sling for a quick attachment.

There are three metal parts to the sling. The hooks, the square slide and the buckle. The best set-up found so far is to have the buckle next to the arm, the square slide in the middle, and the hook on the end to be attached to the swivel. Contrary to exaggerated claims, web slings don't stretch once in position to cause any problems. Life of the web sling is two to three years of hard usage. The first thing to wear will be slippage on the adjustment slide. This can be corrected in the field with a squirt of "Firm Grip" on the offending area of the sling. This will correct the problem for a long time and gives the shooter notice to get a replacement.

The disadvantage of the leather sling is they break keepers, crack, break and become completely useless at the worst time, and further, are a pain to adjust into and out of position. The popularity of the web sling was proven by the number of foreign shooters using the web sling at the Palma International Matches at Raton, NM in 1992. The web sling is not just for beginners, it is also for the advanced shooter— give it a try.
—Mitchell Maxberry

Thanks' Mitch, now a few comments from me. First, the "Purist" would have a cow and protest you if they saw you using a sling with two sets of hooks (for a quick disconnect) in the Off-Hand. "Not As Issued," don't you know. Also <u>it has been declared illegal by NRA & CMP</u>. (I am an NRA Referee.) Second, I will grudgingly admit that if the leather sling should break it will happen at the worst possible time, like just before Rapid Fire. I will also grudgingly admit that the nylon or foreign web sling may have been given the web sling a bad rap.

I respect Mitchell Maxberry's opinion enough to present it here. I do, however, at this stage of my life, prefer to hold onto my pig-headed, illogical, preconceived notions regarding the web sling. Granted, possibly acquired by the use of a nylon or other poor quality sling.

Maybe it would help to understand my views by relating what my daughter Maria, when she was 16 years old, lovingly, told me. "Dad, if you ever got Alzheimer, no one would ever notice."

Oh, by the way, there is a NEW, BETTER way to ASSEMBLE and USE the Service Rifle Sling.

Keep reading, **Chapter Eleven**.

CHAPTER ELEVEN

Jim Owens No-Pulse Service Rifle Sling

Now that you have reviewed the "Conventional" way of using the Leather Service Rifle Sling (Chapter 9), I am now going to show you **a far easier, faster and more efficient technique**. This method of assembling the "No Pulse" sling was conceived by one of my former students and it works far better than any previous "No-Pulse" methods.

What are the advantages of the No-Pulse Sling?

(1) The sling can be placed on your arm, back on the ready line, without handling the rifle, (2) When called to the line, the sling can be attached to the rifle in ten seconds or less, (3) The sling does not slip down on the arm and (4) The sling does not transmit a Pulse Beat to the front sight.

What are the Disadvantages?

Just one, you will need a second sling, such as a web or cotton sling <u>for the Off-Hand Position</u>. Both CMP and NRA rules require that the sling be attached to both the front and rear sling swivel for Off-Hand.

The AWS (All Weather Sling)

So, what makes the No-Pulse sling different than the regular Turner All Weather Synthetic sling?

(1) The AWS has been re-assembled in the No-Pulse configuration,
(2) Both keepers have been replaced with 3-tier larger ones,
(3) The Short Strap is one inch longer to allow the arm hole to be a slightly larger opening for people with larger arms, and
(4) The "D" ring is slightly larger to aid in the assembly.

Can I convert my other Turner Slings to the No-Pulse?

YES, you need Two (2) larger keepers to replace the ones on **the Turner All Weather Synthetic Sling** OR Two (2) larger keepers to replace the "Adjusting" keeper on a **Turner Leather Sling**. I have both types at $7.00 each plus $1.00 S&H. on my web site www.jarheadtop.com

When the No-Pulse Service Rifle Sling first came out, the Range Officer from Hell said "That's Not Legal" ("I have never seen anything like it"). I took it to a couple of members on the CMP (Civilian Marksmanship Program) Rules Committee and said "I can show you six different ways to assemble this sling, this is just one of them, and it has a long strap, a short strap and two keepers. Nothing is added and nothing is taken away."

The CMP said "Wow, that's different, but it is not illegal." I then took it to the Director of CMP, the Director of NRA, and the NRA Referees and they all said the same thing.

If any local *Range Officer from Hell* tries to give you a problem, just tell them what I said. If they insist, tell them you want to file a written protest and contact me. We WILL fight. CMP and NRA have already approved the Turner All Weather Synthetic Sling.

In this chapter I will show you;

1. **How to assemble the sling** (I had my 14-year-old granddaughter assemble it following these pictures and she had no problems).
2. **How to place the sling on your arm.**
3. **How to place the sling on the rifle.**

How to assemble the No-Pulse Sling

Fig. 90

Lay the short strap with the <u>hooks up</u> to your left (Fig. 90).

Fig. 91

Place the two keepers with the staples up and to the left of the hooks (Fig. 91).

Fig. 92

Slide the two keepers over the hooks (Fig. 92)

Fig. 93

Slide the two keepers to the end with the "D" ring (Fig 93).

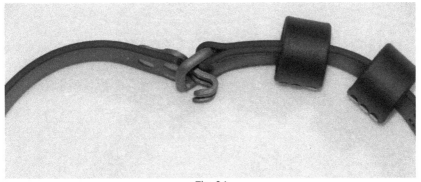

Fig. 94

Form a loop and place the hooks into the "D" ring. Hooks DOWN (Fig. 94)

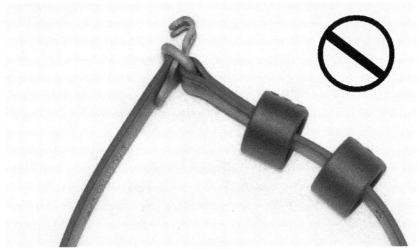

Fig. 95

Here the hooks are shown up (Fig. 95), this is **not correct**, **reverse the loop** as in the picture (Fig 94)

Fig. 96

Pull the hooks through the "D" ring (Fig. 96)

Make sure the "D" ring is facing away from you (The 12 o'clock position). Pull the hooks through the "D" ring about 6-8 inches (Fig. 96).

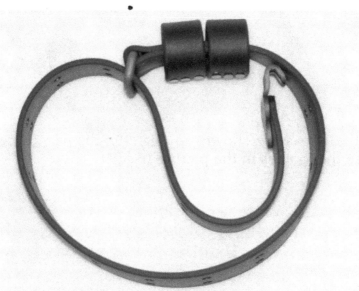

Fig. 97

Bend the hooks back and place them inside the loop (Fig. 97).

IMPORTANT: Look at all the pictures. The "D" ring is at the 12 O'clock position as if it were lying on a table. Make sure you have it done the same.

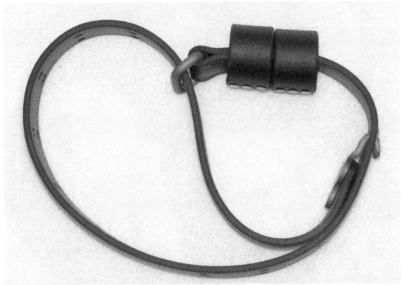

Fig. 98

Move the keepers closer to the "D" ring before putting the hooks in the first set of holes near the keepers (Fig. 98).

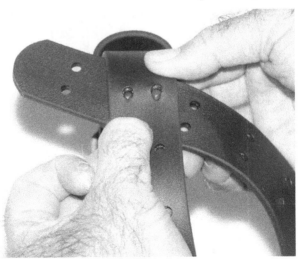

Fig. 99

Use the long strap to cushion your fingers while inserting the hooks (Fig. 99)

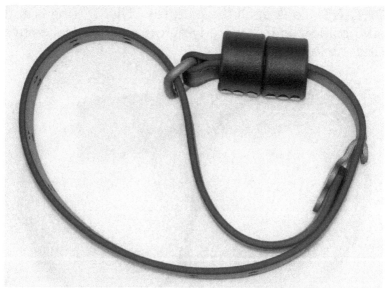

Fig. 100

Place the Hooks into the first set of holes, the ones near the keepers (Fig 100).

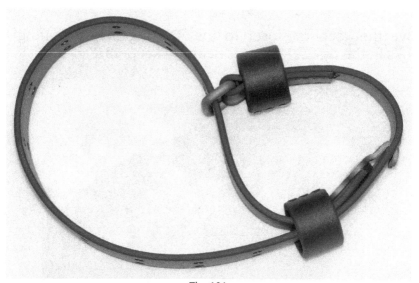

Fig. 101

<u>Slide the first keeper down over the hooks (Fig. 101). The "D" ring is at 12 O'clock and the keepers are to the right</u> Make sure you keep the short strap in this position. This is the correct way. This is very important for both the assembly and

the use of the No-Pulse sling, <u>**ALWAYS make sure the "D" ring is at 12 o'clock and facing AWAY from your body.**</u>

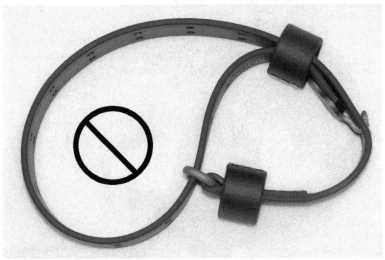

Fig. 102

Here the "D" ring is at 6 O'clock and the keepers are to the right (Fig. 102), **this is not correct**.

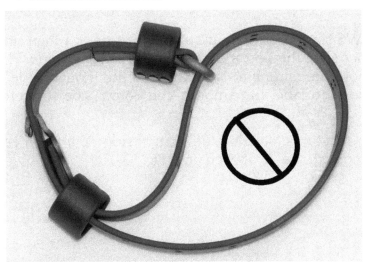

Fig. 103

Here the "D" ring is at 12 O'clock but the keepers are on the left (Fig. 103), <u>**again this is not correct**</u>.

The Long Strap

Fig. 104

The AWS sling does not have a smooth side or rough side. On a leather sling the hooks curl towards the rough side. The side the hooks are curling to is considered the "Rough" side. It is a good idea to label the smooth and rough side for reference later.

In these pictures I labeled the "rough" side "A" at each end and the "smooth" side "B" at each end (Fig. 104).

Fig. 105

Take the long strap with side "A" facing the short strap. The hooks on the **long strap should be facing away from you**.

Feed the long strap into the keeper (Fig. 105), the one at the 6 o'clock position **(Hint: pinch the sides of the keeper together and the strap goes through much easier)**

Fig. 106

Pull the long strap through the keeper until the <u>hooks are about 8-10 inches from the loop or short strap. Notice the hooks on the long strap are facing away from you (Fig. 106)</u>.

Fig. 107

Bring the long strap around to the 2nd keeper. Make sure side "A" is closest to the short strap (Fig. 107)

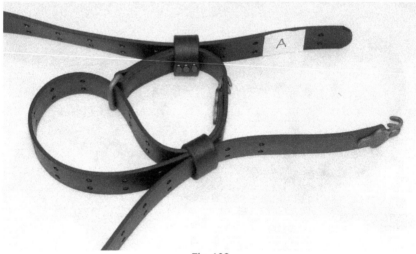

Fig. 108

Feed the end through the 2nd keeper (Fig. 107), again pinching the sides of the keeper makes it easier to slide through.

Fig. 109

Take the sling and lay it on a table like it is shown in the picture above(Fig.109). Make sure the "D" Ring is away from you or at the 12 o'clock position and the keepers are to the **RIGHT**.

If the sling should be flipped over and you notice the "D" Ring is closer to you and is at the 6 o'clock position, **THIS IS THE WRONG WAY TO PLACE IT ON YOUR JACKET** and it will not work. Always make sure the "D" Ring is <u>away from your body</u> and at the 12 o'clock position.

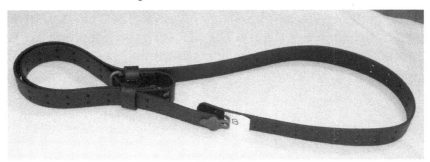

Fig. 110

The sling is now assembled and ready for use (Fig. 110).

Placing the sling on your arm

Fig. 111

In the picture above, the "D" ring is at 12 O'clock and the keepers are on the right. The "D" ring is not close to the bottom keeper and there is slack around the back between the two straps (Fig. 111)

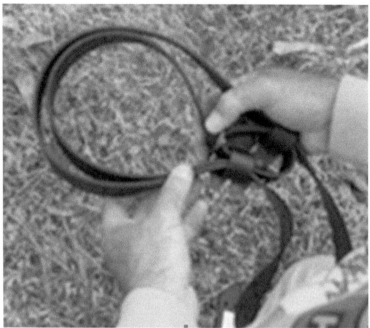

Fig. 112

The "D" ring is now moved down to the bottom keeper, this makes a larger loop for your arm and most of the slack is taken up between the two straps (Fig. 112).

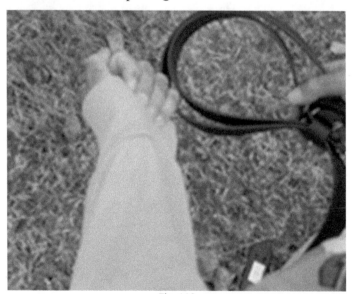

Fig. 113

Holding the sleeve down prevents the coat and sweat shirt from riding up (Fig. 113)

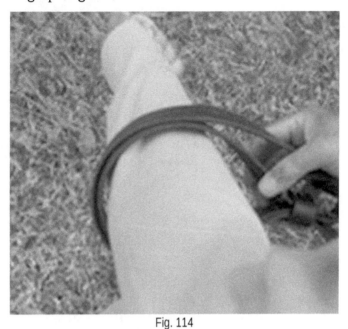

Fig. 114

Slide the arm loop up your left arm (Fig 114).

Fig. 115

Pull the sling up just above the bicep near the arm pit. (Fig. 115).

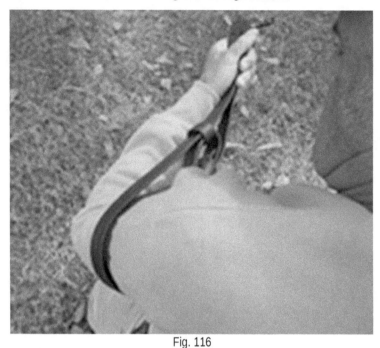

Fig. 116

Hold **_BOTH_** ends of the long strap in your left hand (Fig. 116).

Fig. 117

To make the loop smaller on your arm there are **_TWO_** adjusting points on the short strap. 1) The "D" ring itself and 2) the Lower keeper (Fig. 117).

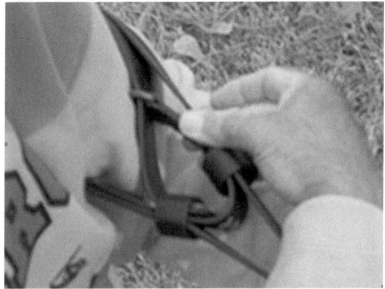
Fig. 118

Bring your left arm tight against your body and start by pushing the "D" ring away from your body (Fig. 118).

Fig. 119

Then push the lower keeper toward your body (Fig. 119).

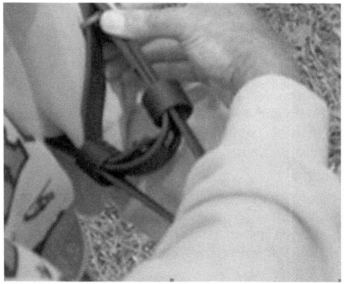
Fig. 120

Back to the "D" ring. At this point push the upper keeper up to the "D" ring.

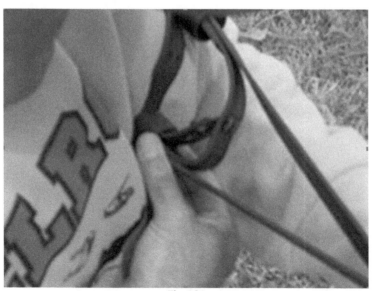
Fig. 121

Then back to the lower keeper (Fig. 121). Simply alternate between pushing the "D" ring away from your body and pushing the lower keeper toward your body.

How tight? When you lower your left hand down along side your body, the small strap will hold on your arm. It does not need to be very tight, just tight enough to keep it from sliding down your arm.

The key to the No-Pulse Sling is that the long strap goes through the lower keep then it **wraps around the back of your arm** then passing through the upper keeper, then through the upper sling swivel finally hooking back onto itself in a set of holes.

When you are down in position, all the pressure is on the back of your arm. Since the sling is not tight on the bicep cutting off the circulation in the arm and thus it does not give a pulse beat that could be transferred through the sling to the front sight post.

You now have the sling on your arm without touching the rifle. This can be done at the ready line while you are waiting to be called to the firing line. When called to the firing line, you can hook up to the rifle in 10 seconds or less.

Attaching the sling to the rifle

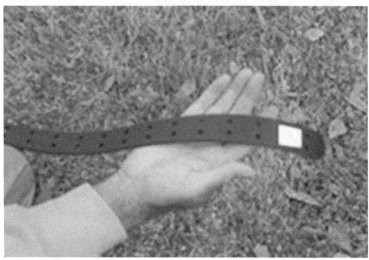

Fig. 122

Lay the sling across the <u>palm of your right hand</u>. Side "B" will be up (Fig. 122).

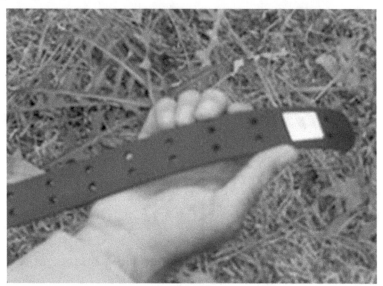

Fig. 123

Place the finger tips of your right hand along the edge of the strap (Fig. 123).

Fig. 124

Push the strap towards you (Fig. 124).

Fig 125

Run the strap **_UP_** through the upper sling swivel and pull it back down as shown (Fig 125).

Fig. 126

Connect the hooks to the end of the strap (Fig 126). Dry firing your position will determine which set of holds to use. You may want to mark the holes in the sling for easier reference.

Fig. 127

The sling will wrap naturally around the back of your hand (Fig. 127).

Remember the rules require the sling be attached to BOTH the upper and lower sling swivels for the Off Hand (Standing) position.

You will not want to disassemble and re-assemble this sling every time. You will need a web or cotton sling for the Off Hand position.

(1) "D" Ring   (2) Adjusting Keeper   (6) Long End

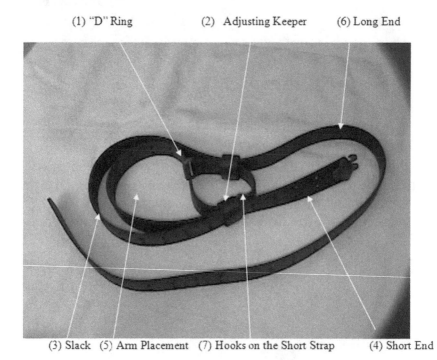

(3) Slack (5) Arm Placement (7) Hooks on the Short Strap   (4) Short End

Fig. 128

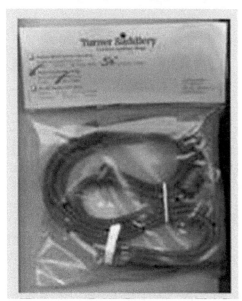

Fig. 129

The "*Jim Owens No-Pulse Sling*" can be purchased (already Fully Assembled) from my web site, www.JarHeadTop.com.

ABOUT THE AUTHOR

In 1963, when Jim joined the Marine Corps, he had no experience with firearms. One of the Drill Instructors wore an Expert Badge, that's Jim's primary recollection of him. The EXPERT MARKSMANSHIP MEDAL hanging on his chest—and Jim wanted one just like it! Jim came home from boot camp carrying his first of many Marksmanship trophies—and wearing the gleaming silver EXPERT BADGE!

During his Marine Corps career, he acted as coach and firing member of the Marksmanship Training Unit at MCAS, Cherry Point, N.C. He's fired in the Eastern, Far Eastern, Western and Pacific Marine Corps Division Matches. (Each of these matches includes one week of classes. Thus, Jim has over 500 hours of classroom training, over and above the firing line experience.)

In 1968, Jim had the opportunity to try out for the Olympic Pistol Team. The final stage of that competition is 4 SECONDS OF PURE PANIC! Jim hit two targets, a paste bucket and a score keeper. It was somewhere in that time frame that Jim realized that rifle shooting was his forte. Jim was also a Marksmanship Instructor at the U. S. Naval Academy.

He went on to become coach, as well as firing member of base teams at MCB, Camp Pendleton, CA and MCB, Quantico, VA for the Inter-service and National Matches in 1981 and 1983. In 1982 he coached the winning six man Team in the All Marine Corps Championships.

In his shooting career, he's earned 3 Bronze Legs, 1 Silver Leg, 1 Gold Leg and a Distinguished Badge. He's a High Master and a member of the 495 Club.

Since retiring as a M/SGT in 1986, Jim's been actively engaged in promoting excellence in the sport and civilian participation in Competitive High Power Shooting. He uses Racine County Line Rifle Club (WI) as his home base and experimental lab.

To ward off winter BLAH's (a.k.a. "Range's Snowed Over!"), in 1988, at the urging of Bob Schanen, Jim began holding Feb. – Apr. classes in technique, personal training, equipment handling, etc. From those humble beginnings (6 men in Bob's basement) evolved what in 1992 equaled in excess of 100 participants (men, women and juniors) in a two-phase (Basic and Advanced) training program.

For more information on holding Marksmanship Training classes in your area, call or write:

Jim Owens
112 Red Wing Dr.
Enterprise, AL 36330
(334) 347-0020

Shooting Products
from Jim Owens

Sight Alignment, Trigger Control & The Big Lie

A Power-packed book that has helped many shooters improve their groups and scores, some by as much as forty or fifty points. This book covers not only the basics of breathing, natural point of aim, sight alignment, sight picture, focus and trigger control exercises. It has sections on Mental conditioning, marking the sights, zeroing, normal come ups, light effects, damage to the crown, care in cleaning, throat erosion and bullet run out. There is also an advanced theory that has been praised by High Masters and Marksmen.
- *Now in Paperback & Ebook versions* -

New CD version includes a new chapter **"Analyzing Groups"** with more and better pictures for the price of the book. Yes, you may print off pages as you need them for the range!
 $14.95 plus $2.80 S&H

Reading the Wind and Coaching Techniques

To excel in any outdoor shooting sport you will need to learn how to compensate for the effects of the wind. Jim Owens' 20+ years of Marine Corps Shooting Team experience will give you the knowledge of how to read, judge and adjust for the wind—in any type of rifle competition.

You'll learn a simple system for judging the speed, direction and value of the wind. You'll learn to read the mirage, how to accurately read the range flag, estimate wind speed, wind strategies, effects on the bullet and much more. Also included are 22 <u>sets</u> of wind charts for a variety of calibers (.223, .308, 6.5-08, 6.5-284, .300 Win. Mag.), bullet weights, and for **both** Across the course and Long Range. 80 wind charts in total!
- *In Ebook & Paperback (Jan. 2015) versions* -

Now on CD too, in an easy to use PDF format, more and better pictures for the price of the book. Yes, you may print off pages as you need them for the range!
 $12.95 plus $2.80 S&H

Care, Cleaning and Sportsmanship

The Care and Cleaning of Rifles, with particular attention to the Service Rifles. Tips on Bullet Seating, An interview, Questions & Answers with Boots Obermeyer, Jack Krieger, Charlie Milazzo and Mike Bykowski. Also, Interviews with Seven National Champions as how they clean their bores. An extensive chapter on "Moly Coating." The positive side of Sportsmanship.
$12.95 plus $2.80 S&H

"FOUR BOOK SET"

Get all four books at a special reduced rate! *Save $5.85*
"Reading the Wind and Coaching Techniques", "Sight Alignment, Trigger Control and the Big Lie", "Leather Sling and Shooting Positions", "Care, Cleaning and Sportsmanship"

All four together on CD, with all the added chapters and wind charts from each individual book as well as all the newer and better pictures!
$43.95 plus $5.40 S&H

Advance Theory CD

For many years shooters have made a sight adjustment and have come out the other side. Someone would tell them, "you must put one click on the rifle and one click in your head". The "Windage and Elevation" rule states, "One click will move the strike of the bullet one inch per 100 yards. Jim's Advance Theory says, You must do two things with it: (1) Memorize it, because people will talk about it, and (2) Forget it, it does not work!
Jim gives you an alternate theory in three Power Point Presentations on the CD - That Does Work!
And, get Personal Support after viewing the CD! If you have any questions or do not understand something, just call Jim at 334-347-0020 and he will be more than happy to help you.
$20 plus $2.20 S&H

Reading The Wind 2 CD Set

The first CD has Jim's *"Reading the Wind"* that he uses in his classes; the most recent and best efforts.
Included:

- Different forces affecting the bullet
- A simple system anyone can use to "Read The Wind"
- Simple and inexpensive aides to help you
- A detailed description as to reading the mirage
- A simple and the most accurate way to read flags

◆ "Alternative" methods when the mirage or flags are not readable

The second CD has 22 Sets of really good Wind Charts - PLUS a bonus short class on using Kentucky Windage.
$25 plus $3.50 S&H

Line & Pit Procedures CD

When we 1st participate in a new sport we are a little intimidated. We don't know what to expect. We do not want to make a mistake, look foolish, maybe having someone yell at us or mess someone else up.

Well, come along with me. We are going to a High Power Rifle Match. We are going from start to finish. From the time we arrive at the Range, to checking in at the stat office, getting assigned our relay, dropping our gear off at the ready line and reporting to the Pits. •We are going to be there all day. We will see the different relays fire the Match and in turn see the different problems that can come up and how they are handled. •We are going to find out where to go and when. We will find out what we have to do when we get there and what supplies we will need. We will find out the proper way to run a target, both in slow fire and rapid fire. How to handle the different situations. •We will learn the Range Commands, both Line and The Pits. We will learn the flow of the Match.
I am going to show you some of the small tricks I have learned in over 45 years of shooting. **$11.95 plus $2.20 S&H**

Score Keeping CD

You learn by doing! After the instruction phase you actually score a shooter in both slow fire and rapid fire. The different problems that can occur will be presented as you score the shooter. You will get years of experience in a single setting. In fact, you will know more than most people that have been shooting 5 to 10 years.
$11.95 plus $2.20 S&H

The Complete AR-15 High Performance Guide

The latest on accuracy modifications and accessories for "Space Guns" and Service Rifles. It features an extensive hand loading section and shooting techniques specifically suited to the AR-15. It also includes special chapters with 11-time Champion G. David Tubb on the AR-10/SR-25; USAMU head C.I. Boyd and ace shooter Sgt. Lew Tippie; gunsmith Derrick Martin; and the input of a dozen other industry leaders! Written by a High Master Service Rifle Shooter, critics have said it is one of the finest books they've ever read on the subject of High Power Rifle Competition.
$28.95 plus $5.40 S&H

Hand loading for Competition

A brand new book by the author and publisher of The Competitive AR15.

It's a guide to "practical precision" in producing high-performance ammunition.
$ 34.95 plus $5.40 S&H

Jim Owens Data Book
Some of the features are Eight Sets of Wind Charts, A Wind Speed
Estimating Guide, More than Twice the # of pages., Larger plotting areas, All
Scoring rings are Proportional, Jim Owens "Amended" grid lines, Twin
plotting bulls for rapid fire, A "Gun Round Count" page, A Check list for items
to bring to the range, A chart detailing the scores needed for each
classification, A chart giving the dimensions of the scoring rings, A chart
describing the scoring system, A guide for normal come-ups from 100 to
1,000 yards in 100 yard increments, A chart explaining the "9-Yes, 9-No"
problems. This data book is more than a $60.00 value.
$15.95 Plus $5.40 S&H. Sent via Priority Mail

NEW - *Use of the Jim Owens Data Books*
$15.00 plus S&H or $10.00 plus S&H if ordered with any data book!

Jim Owens (Long Range) Data Book
Some of the features are: 54 two sided pages for the 600 yard stage and 54
two sided pages for the 800/900/1,000 yard target, 14 Sets of Wind Charts, A
Wind Speed Estimating Guide, Larger plotting areas, All Scoring rings are
Proportional, Jim Owens "Amended" grid lines, A "Gun Round Count" page,
A chart detailing the scores needed for each classification, A chart giving the
dimensions of the scoring rings, A chart describing the scoring system, A
guide for normal come-ups from 100 to 1,000 yards in 100 yard increments.
$15.95 Plus $5.40 S&H. Sent via Priority Mail

Jim Owens
112 Red Wing Dr.
Enterprise, AL 36330
334-347-0020
Top@JarHeadTop.com
www.JarHeadTop.com

What they are saying about
Sight Alignment, Trigger Control & The Big Lie
by Jim Owens

"My scores have improved drastically. I thank you for your books. High Power shooting is enjoyable when you do better."
    —Neal Trubitt

"After shooting my first match a few weeks ago. One of the guys from my club loaned me a set of your books. I can not thank you enough. I can under-stand what you are talking about. I know the next match will go much better for me. Thanks Again"
    —John DeMoss

"Your series of books and tapes have helped me make the first daunting steps and I entered my first competitive event ever, the 2004 NRA High Power Week Competition at Camp Perry. Your Data Book is the best that I have seen and all the information that you had put together and your per-sonal commitment to Juniors in the sport is indeed commendable."
    —Steven Field

"Your books were so great and helpful, I gave them to my Dad, and have not seen them back! So I need another set!"
    —Another happy customer

CPSIA information can be obtained
at www.ICGtesting.com
Printed in the USA
BVHW041324271218
536524BV00017B/131/P